50001388770 5

C000186862

Beaufighter Over the Balkans

Beaufighter Over the Balkans

From the Balkans Air Force to the Berlin Airlift

Steve Stevens DFC

Pen & Sword
AVIATION

First published in Great Britain in 2006 by
PEN & SWORD AVIATION
an imprint of
Pen & Sword Books Limited
47 Church Street
Barnsley
S. Yorkshire
S70 2AS

ISBN 1 84415 487 4
ISBN 978 1 84415 487 6

A CIP catalogue record for this book
is available from the British Library.

Printed and bound in Great Britain
by CPI UK

Pen & Sword Books Ltd incorporates the imprints of
Pen & Sword Aviation, Pen & Sword Maritime,
Pen & Sword Military, Wharncliffe Local History, Pen & Sword Select,
Pen & Sword Military Classics and Leo Cooper.

For a complete list of Pen & Sword titles please contact:
PEN & SWORD BOOKS LIMITED
47 Church Street, Barnsley, South Yorkshire, S70 2AS, England.
E-mail: enquiries@pen-and-sword.co.uk
Website: www.pen-and-sword.co.uk

Dedication

I dedicate this book to the memory of those who died. As an WWII Air Force veteran I particularly think of the 'few' who fought so brilliantly and courageously in the air, in the Battle of Britain.

Deep in my memory are those courageous airmen of Bomber Command who knew that every time they took off they would probably not return.

Naturally, those I knew who died through enemy Ack-Ack guns, are those who I often think about. Dicky Dickson, my fellow Beaufighter pilot with No. 19 South African Air Force Squadron, who, with the rest of us, survived our sinking of the SS *Kuckuck*, but a few days later when the rest of us got back, he was shot down and killed when we attacked Cernick Castle.

Then too, there is Eric Impey. On the day of his first supply drop over Warsaw, he knew that with the terrifically high losses, that he might not get back. So that day he wrote a poem. It has been called *An Airmen's Prayer* and ranks among the most famous poems of WWII. He was a four-engined Liberator pilot with No. 31 SAAF. He and his crew were shot down over Warsaw that night and none survived. The six verses of his poem are included in this book. Here is how it ends.

And should it be my time to die.
Be with me to the end.
Help me to die a Christian's death.
On Thee, God, I depend.
Then as I leave this mortal frame
from human ties set free,
Receive my soul O God of love.
I humbly come to Thee.

5

Photographs

*I*t is said 'A Picture is Worth a Thousand Words'. That's been my aim. That is why the photos carry a comment. Sometimes, where the full story is not told in the text, a long description is right there with the photo.

A large proportion of 'Action Photos' are in the chapters on our rocket firing Beaufighter air-strikes over the Balkans. That is because for strategic and tactical reasons, we had wonderful cameras in the noses of our Beaus. The film would start rolling whenever we pressed our 20mm cannon firing button or our rocket firing button. There was also a camera starting switch which the pilot could use to start the film rolling at an appropriate time. But, in the heat of battle when Ack-Ack guns had begun or were about to attempt to shoot us down it was hard to remember to use that switch. Steve Schonveldt, who often flew as my number two, and I, who were both keen photographers usually managed to remember and planned ahead of our attacks when we would start our film rolling. That's how Steve planned and took the famous photo of my rockets being fired at Zuzemberk. That's why the photos in the Balkan Air Force chapters are some of the most outstanding air-strike photos of WWII.

The Beaufighter's nose camera

Contents

The photo opposite of me firing my eight rockets from my No. 19 Squadron, South African Air Force Beaufighter has become one of the famous Second World War photos. What, however, is virtually unknown is how it came to be taken.

In February 1945 the Yugoslav Partisans were intent on ousting the Germans from their village of Zuzemberk, which was a local Nazi HQ. They asked if the Balkan Air Force would blitz their village at lunchtime when they hoped the Nazi soldiers would let up on their vigilant watch for a Partisan attack that was always a possibility. The date requested was the 13th. Usually the Partisans would request that our Beaufighters destroy a specific building. But not this time. All they wanted was for us to fire our rockets anywhere into the village – except at their church – to cause pandemonium.

The Partisans informed us that they would be close by in hiding in a forest facing the massive medieval castle-like walls that had been built all those years ago on that side of the village. On hearing our planes approaching they would rush out of the forest and cross the freezing cold fast-flowing but shallow river, and skirt around the walls to a place where they hoped to be able to storm the village.

The Balkan Air Force asked our squadron to take this on. We decided to use eight Beaufighters. A section of four was to make their attack on one side of the village. I as leader of the other section took on the other side of the village.

As we had not been requested to strike any particular buildings there was no need to make a customary very low-level extremely dangerous attack.

Steve Schonveld and I were keen photographers. Unlike most of the other pilots we usually used our nose-camera tumbler-switch on our control column to set the film in our camera moving as we approached our target, to be sure we took as many photos as possible with these great cameras. Once set in motion they took photos' automatically until the film ran out, whenever we used the tumbler-switch or were set going when we pressed the button of our cannon or our rocket button.

Steve Schonveld, when he saw the village, suddenly saw an opportunity for a great photo. He got himself into the exact position where he could see through his gun sight, my Beaufighter and the village. In this position, which was guesswork as we had never tried a photo like this before, he waited a few seconds until he saw my rockets leaving the rails on the underside of my planes' wings and flicked the tumbler switch.

He had forgotten one thing. I would be pressing and holding down the cannon button to fire my four 20 mm cannons before firing my rockets. The large empty shells hit his aircraft. When he parked his plane back at our Italian Adriatic coastal air base, which we knew as Biferno because of the river, or Termoli because of the little nearly ancient village of Termoli, his mechanics at his parking bay were not very pleased when they saw the dents the empty shells had made on the wings of their Beaufighter.

A few days later we were informed that the Partisans had successfully routed the enemy and had retaken their town. So that is the story of that famous photo. The accounts of some of our other rocket attacks and other great photos will appear elsewhere in this book.

I think Steve Schonveld's ground crew forgave him for damaging their Beaufighter when they saw this amazing photo.

Foreword

*I*n the past decade a number of good and excellent books have been published about the South African Air Force. However, the majority have been written with the aircraft as central theme. It is thus refreshing to read of the human side in *Beaufighter over the Balkans* by Steve Stevens, DFC, SAAF.

The author, who served a decade in the South African Air Force, weaves an interesting story of a young man growing up to serve his country as an active pilot in time of war. Rather than a factual, technical type book, he has taken his memories and experiences and written his own personal story around the many people he knew: his long time friends, colleagues and acquaintances. The text reads well and good photographs illustrate the story. The book thus gives a different dimension to the history of the South African Air Force.

I have had the privilege of meeting a few of those mentioned in his book. This is what *Beaufighter over the Balkans* brought to me - the human side, the people, the characters. It is a tangible and historic connection between man, machine and environment.

With limited financial resources the South African Air Force is not able to publish historic books. In effect it is left to a handful of dedicated authors, such as Steve, and researchers to record for posterity the stories and anecdotes of aircraft, and the men and women of the South African Air Force. I am of the opinion that there are many who served in the South African Air Force with a story to tell, and who like Steve could add one small moment in time to the rich history of the South African Air Force. It is these stories that need to be told and recorded for the future generation South African Air Force.

Throughout the book Steve gives credit to our Creator for watching over him during the foolhardy escapes to the danger fraught missions. It was a refreshing experience to read of the Man, Steve Stevens and his commitment. From the poem *High Flight* by John G. Magee I highlight two lines:

Oh, I have slipped the surly bonds of earth…
Put out my hand, and touched the face of God

I commend this book to all who love the thrill of flight and to Steve for writing about a small yet important facet of personal life in the history of South African Air Force.

Brigadier General Derrick Page, SM*, MMM*, SAAF
Director Air Force Heritage
South African Air Force

October 2006

Introduction

*S*ome time ago a friend of mine, who has a considerable knowledge of aviation, saw some of the amazing photos that I, and some of my pilot colleagues, took with the cameras in the noses of our twin-engined rocket-firing Beaufighters.

These photos were taken in 1944 and 1945, when I was a pilot with the South African Air Force (SAAF). I was serving with 19 SAAF Squadron at Biferno, halfway up the leg of Italy, on the Adriatic coast. Our squadron was one of the many squadrons based along the Adriatic that were part of the newly formed Balkan Air Force. Our task was to work with the Yugoslav Partisans to drive the Germans out of the Balkans.

My friend Kenneth Hearn, who was the honorary representative for Mission Aviation Fellowship in Sussex, said he was sure that some of Britain's leading aviation magazines, which were publishing Second World War photographic articles, would publish some from me. I decided to give it a try.

One photo in my collection had become one of the most famous Beaufighter rocket-firing air strike photos of Second World War. It was taken by my fellow pilot and friend, Steve Schonveld, my No. 2. He had been able to position his plane in exactly the right position to take this great photo. It captured the moment when my eight 4 ft (1.2m) rockets, with their 60 lb. warheads, left the rocket rails under my wings.

Steve Stevens

I wrote an article about this particular attack, which was made on the small fortress town of Zuzemberk, utilised then as a Nazi HQ. It was a decisive event that made it possible for the Yugoslav Partisans to defeat the Nazis. *Aviation Monthly* published my long article unabridged, with the dramatic photo appearing on a full page. Since then it has been published elsewhere, including *Amateur Photographer*, which published it as a double-page tear-out spread.

This initial success spurred me on to write further photographic articles. Three were published in *Flypast*, Britain's top-selling aviation monthly magazine, in *Aviation Illustrated* and in *Air Pictorial*. Still others are in preparation. A book publisher then suggested that I write a flying autobiography. This is it.

Rather than writing it as a technical book for aviators, I have intended this book for the general public, who may only have a fleeting interest in flying. I have highlighted the dramatic – and often foolhardy – events of my wartime flying career in their historic context. Some embarrassed me then – and still do when they come to mind sixty years later!

Why did I survive, when so many of my fine fellow aviators died? This is something I have thought about many, many times, especially as I was often so foolhardy. I trust the reader will find the answer in this book, although there is no easy answer to such a question.

Why, for example, did Eric Impey die over Warsaw, the night after he had written his amazing poem? And yet his friend, Bryan Jones, with whom he shared a tent, survived. Bryan was flying as the navigator of a four-engined Liberator, whose engines were shot out. The plane managed to land itself on the only open space in Warsaw, in a pitch-dark night.

My account of my flying to Berlin over a hundred times during the 1948/9 Berlin Airlift is included in this account of flying in war. Even though the 'hot war' was over at that time, we were in a 'cold war' with the Soviet Union. It could easily have led to the Third World War, if we had not been miraculously successful.

High Flight

Oh, I have slipped the surly bonds of earth
And danced the skies on laughter-silvered wings;
Sunward I've climbed, and joined the tumbling mirth
Of sun-split clouds – and done a hundred things
You have not dreamed of – wheeled and soared and swung
High in the sunlit silence;
Hov'ring there, I've chased the shouting wind along,
And flung my eager craft through footless halls of air.
Up, up the long delirious burning blue,
I've topped the windswept heights with easy grace
Where never lark, or even eagle flew,
And, while with silent, lifting mind I've trod
The high untrespassed sanctity of space,
Put out my hand, and touched the face of God.

John Gillespie Magee Jnr
3 September 1941

This expresses – quite wonderfully – how many of us felt.

CHAPTER 1

Second World War Commences: Cape Town

When war broke out in 1939, I was a twenty-year-old in Cape Town studying for Christian service at the Bible Institute of South Africa. We had just moved from our old and inadequate premises in the suburb of Mowbray to our newly built premises at Kalk Bay, overlooking the little fishing harbour. At first the war in Europe seemed rather remote and life went on as normal.

Close shave in the Boomslang Caves

I would often sit studying at my table, looking out of the window at the sea. It was an idyllic setting. I was later moved to a back room. Now my window overlooked the mountains. Being a farm boy, I loved the open spaces. The lovely mountain that I was looking at was the extension of the Devil's Peak, part of the famous Table Mountain. I had found that if one turned a photo or picture postcard of Table Mountain on its side, then Devil's Peak had the distinct appearance of an evil-looking face.

I had been informed that somewhere within my gaze that mountain was riddled with caves. One day, when I had some free time, I set off to look for them. I had a box of matches in my pocket and an inch or two of an almost burnt-out candle. After a lot of searching through the bushy undergrowth, I saw a hole and, flat on my stomach, I began edging my way forward. As I progressed, the opening gradually became smaller and smaller. I soon realised that it would be dangerous to go any further. I could not even get my hands into my pocket to get my matches and candle to strike a light to look ahead.

My grandfather, Lt Col Stephen John Stevens, who I was named after. He was almost killed after being shot in the jaw in the Lotuli bush by Xhosa warriors during the 1877–81 war.

It was not until I decided to retreat that I realised that it is one thing to move forward on one's stomach, but very much harder to move backwards! It took me a long time to get back. It was a great relief when I finally freed myself and sat in the warm African sun, regaining my composure.

Soon however, I found another small opening. Lighting my candle, I made my way forward.

1940. All about to join the SAAF as volunteers. Left to right: Rory Douglas became a pilot (killed); Deryck Radford joined the Medical Corps and became a doctor; John Poorter SAAF air photographer trainee, became a minister with a doctorate (we married sisters); myself; and squatting, David McPhail, joined the army. All apart from Rory were Bible Institute of SA students at the time.

Suddenly I found myself in a large cavern. I had been told that it was possible to find a way to the top of the mountain in those Boomslang Caves. ('Boomslang' means 'tree snake' in afrikaans.)

So I started exploring this large cavern. I found a number of openings, but with so little of my candle left, I did not venture far. When I decided that I had had enough, I began looking for the way out. To my dismay, I was not at all sure which of the openings was the one I had come in by. My lighted candle was getting smaller and smaller. And I had not told anyone where I was going. I realised that if I could not find my way out before my candle ran out, I might die in that cavern. As those caves were rarely explored, I would probably not be found until my body was a skeleton. It was a great relief when I did eventually find my way out. Never had daylight been so sweet. That was my last excursion into the Boomslang Caves!

South Africans join up

By the time 1940 arrived, the war in Europe was much in our thoughts and in our prayers. Troop ships were arriving at Cape Town's harbour, carrying Australians, New Zealanders and other Commonwealth-country soldiers to England. Trained troops were also going the other way: to Abyssinia (now Ethiopia) and beyond to North Africa.

The reports from the BBC about these events, together with the stirring speeches from Winston Churchill, touched our consciences. We students, too, began to think that we should be involved.

Ian Knight, the well known Zulu historian, identified this shield from the Battle of Isandlwana, where my grandfather's regiment was almost wiped out. The spears are from the Xhosas.

THE BIBLE INSTITUTE
OF SOUTH AFRICA

KALK BAY, CAPE TOWN

This Diploma certifies that

S. J. Stevens

has completed as a diligent student, to the satisfaction of the Faculty, the Course of Biblical, Theological and Practical Subjects prescribed by this Institute; and has during that period given clear evidence of a true Christian Character, and of ability and willingness to work harmoniously with others and to submit to recognised authority.

Given at Kalk Bay this __16th__ day of *August*

in the year of our Lord __1940.__

Joseph Ward.
Principal.

F. J. Peters
Chairman.

Chas. F. Laurs
Hon. Secretary.

Our college closed in 1940 for the duration of the war, when some of us felt we should volunteer to fight for freedom.

Although South Africa was backing the war effort, there was no conscription. However, large numbers of South Africa's young white men were volunteering.

Those with a British background wanted to help their motherland. Afrikaners with a Dutch background volunteered because they were distressed that the Nazis had taken Holland. Later we were told that the percentage of volunteers from the Afrikaans-speaking Orange Free State was higher than that from English-speaking Natal.

First we talked together as students, then with our faculty. After much discussion and prayer, it was decided that the college would close for the duration of the war. Many of us had only studied for eighteen months of our two-year course. But we left with our diplomas.

With high hopes of becoming a pilot in the South African Air Force, I caught the train for the 1,000-mile (1,600 km) journey to Pretoria. It was not many hours after boarding the train at Cape Town that our two steam engines began struggling to pull the carriages up and through the mountains. We eventually reached the plateau at well over 2,000 ft (600 km) above sea level.

We had arrived in the Small Karoo. Some hours later we were in the Great Karoo, where my father was farming. I had decided to break my journey there – halfway to Pretoria – to say goodbye, not knowing what my future would hold.

The Miracle of Dunkirk

Although it is difficult to recall our thinking of what moved us most during those early days of the Second World War, I think it must have been the miracle of Dunkirk. Although it happened well over sixty years ago and thousands of miles from where I was at that time, it often comes flooding back into my memory.

The full impact of that miracle only dawned on me many years later when I read one of the three short volumes of the Rev. David Gardner's books under the general title of The Trumpet Sounds for Britain. Here is the substance of David Gardner's research of Dunkirk 1940.

At the request of His Majesty King George VI, Sunday 26 May was observed as a National Day of Prayer. The King in a stirring broadcast called the people of Britain and the Empire to commit their cause to God. The following day, the German High Command announced: 'The British Army is encircled and our troops are proceeding to its annihilation.'

At that time Churchill said:

> *I thought – and some good judges agreed with me – that perhaps*
> *20,000 to 30,000 men might be re-embarked... the whole root and*
> *core and brain of the British army... seemed about to perish upon*
> *the field, or to be led into captivity.*

Then three miracles happened after that National Day of Prayer:

Hitler stopped his general advance.

A storm of extraordinary fury grounded the German Air Force on 28 May.

A great calm settled over the English Channel for several days.

When Churchill announced the miracle of Dunkirk in the House of Commons, his voice was charged with emotion when he said: '335,000 men have been carried out of the jaws of death and shame, to their native land.'

The following Sunday – 9 June 1940 – services of national thanksgiving were held in all churches. The first National Day of Prayer in the Second World War had brought a miracle of deliverance.

CHAPTER 2

Days on Our Farm

*M*y father met me at Cradock railway station. As we drove the ten miles to our farm, I told him that I had ambitions of becoming a pilot. I wondered how he would take that.

Some months before war broke out, I had heard that the SAAF in Cape Town was prepared to allow young fellows to fly in one of its planes. But if we was under twenty-one years of age, we had to have a death warrant signed by our next of kin. In the event of our death in an accident, there would then be no claim against the SAAF. I had sent a copy to my father to sign, but he had refused. He felt flying was too dangerous.

Now that there was war, he no longer felt that way. He had himself served in the First World War as an officer with the West Yorkshire Regiment and had been gassed in Salonika. In fact we only emigrated to South Africa in 1929, when I was ten years old.

At that time he was serving with his regiment in Northern Ireland and they were about to be moved to India. His medical officer did not think he would survive in India, so he was invalided out. We – my father, mother and I, their only child – went to South Africa to save his life in a warm and dry country.

My days on the farm, before going on to Pretoria to join up, were days of reflection and enjoying being on the farm once again. After my mother died in Natal, where my Dad bought his first South African farm, he

My father, George Alexander Stevens, who was trained at Sandhurst. He served in World War One with the West Yorkshire Regiment and was gassed in Salonika. He was invalided out in 1929 and we went to South Africa to save his life in a dry, hot climate.

sold up and went to Johannesburg for the sake of my education. He then became ill and nearly died. That resulted in my leaving college. Instead he bought a farm in the Great Karoo, where the climate would suit his lung condition.

I worked on that farm for three years, until I felt that I did not want to spend my life working with sheep and cattle, but with people instead. As I look back, I believe my going to the Bible Institute was one of the best things I've ever done. Those eighteen months gave me the Christian foundation for a long life in God's service.

The Great Fish River

During this time out before the start of my military service, I roamed all over the farm once again. I was eating navel oranges picked from trees in our orchard, ripe figs that were wonderfully sweet and huge, and pomegranates filled with large pips. One day I went down to the Great Fish River at the bottom of our farm. Standing on the high bank, I looked down about 50 ft (15m) to a trickle of water. All the water had been tapped out for irrigation purposes.

I then recalled the day when I was riding my horse, intending to cross the river, only to find it in flood due to heavy rains miles away to the north. The swirling muddy water looked ominous. I still thought, though, that my brave and strong little horse would be able to swim against the current and get us safely across.

When we reached the middle of the river, I found the current was much stronger than I expected. Nevertheless, my fine steed had his head and eyes firmly fixed on the cutting, which was the only way out of that raging torrent. He battled hard against the current and made it. Had he failed we would probably have drowned, as the next cutting was not for another mile or two downstream.

As my thoughts wandered back to that day, I wished he were still around. I then recalled the subsequent events, when all the horses and mules on our farm contracted a deadly disease. When my father and I saw that nothing could be done for them, I had loaded our rifle and shot first the mules and horses, who were lying in their paddock with their heads flat on the ground from exhaustion.

I had then walked to the stable, where I found my super little mottled blue-grey horse in the same position. When he heard me coming, he struggled to move his head to meet my gaze. His eye met mine and seemed to be pleading for help. He would have heard those four shots ringing out. Perhaps he knew instinctively what was coming. Was he pleading for me not to shoot him? I'll never know. It was with a heavy heart that I shot him and put him out of his misery.

Mountain-top igloo tomb

If he had still been alive, I would have ridden my horse to the foot of the mountain behind us. I would have tethered him to a tree and climbed to the top, to see once again one particular, small, igloo-shaped tomb made of stone. Olive Schriener, the South African author, had probably written her book *Life on a South African Farm* in an old farm house on the banks of the Great Fish River, less than a mile from where I was standing now. She had asked to be buried, with her dog, up on that mountain.

I also would have liked to find out if a colony of baboons were still living there. When I had previously climbed that mountain, it was not even necessary to see or hear them to know they were there. I had been able to tell of their presence by observing some of the thousands of small, flat stones about a foot square in size. The baboons sometimes raided the farms at night looking for food. But they lived mainly on prickly pear that grew all over the mountain, and scorpions, which they would find under those stones. Whenever there was evidence that stones had been recently moved, I knew the baboons were still in hiding somewhere on that mountain.

Goodbyes

My leisurely days on the farm soon came to an end. It was time to say goodbye to all the people working on the farm: the servants and all the members of the Sparks family. Levisse and Maria Sparks had six daughters, most of whom were employed in the Christian guest-house that my father and stepmother were running on that farm.

My father was now married to one of the nurses from Murchison Mission Hospital in Natal. It was the same nurse who had looked after my mother. My father and stepmother now had three small children.

The Sparks were a mixed-race family. Their family probably descended from black women who had been made pregnant by white sailors, whose ships would stop at Cape Town, East London or Port Elizabeth to replenish their supplies.

Maria Sparks was a wonderful cook. Her daughters were lovely girls. We got to know them well, because we saw them every day around the house. We became very close to them and have never lost touch with them.

CHAPTER 3

Joining the South African Air Force

*S*oon I was once again on the train, this time for another 500 miles (800 km). Again we were on the climb, from 2,500 feet above sea level to nearly 6,000 (760 – 1,800 m). When I got off the train at Pretoria, I made my way to Roberts Heights.

It so happened that one of the Bible College students, by the name of John Poorter, was on guard duty when I arrived. He had joined up as an air photographer. That seemed like a good idea for my own career, as I was very keen on photography. If I was turned down as a pupil pilot, I thought I would apply to be mustered as an air photographer.

After my medical, where I was passed as A1, I made my application for training as a SAAF pilot. However, I was turned down, as I had left school early and had not matriculated. So I joined the SAAF as an air photographer and was sent down to the nearby Zwartkops aerodrome, where I was given tests, which included questions on developing film.

I joined the SAAF as a trainee air photographer in 1940 but within months remustered as aircrew.

My score was 7 out of 10, which meant I had passed and would be paid 7 shillings a day. I kicked myself for not getting a score of 8 and therefore 8 shillings a day. The question that tipped the balance had been: what would you do about a red stain? The easy answer was: use a red filter. An extra shilling a day would have been very welcome, but as a tradesman who had passed a test, I was still well off. Most of the other fellows were only getting half that!

The miracle of the Battle of Britain

At this time – being so far away from Britain – we knew very little about what was taking place in Europe. Later on we realised that while we were at what was then known as Robert's Heights, near Pretoria, the Nazis were on the brink of conquering Britain.

It was not until much later that we learnt that Hitler did not follow on after Dunkirk to cross the Channel and invade Britain, whose army had lost all its weapons. He continued to hesitate all through June 1940, giving Britain a breathing space. Air Chief Marshal Sir Hugh

Dowding, Commander-in-Chief of Fighter Command, was asked 'What are your plans for defeating an overwhelming number of the German Air Force?' He replied, 'I believe in God. And there is radar.'

Field Marshal Goering told his air commander that the way ahead for launching an invasion was to destroy the Royal Air Force.

It was later we heard that on 30 August, when we were 'chafing at the bit', wanting to be involved in action, the Battle of Britain had begun. On that day 800 enemy aircraft attacked key airfields in southern England. Within a week Fighter Command was in serious trouble. Aircraft and pilots were being lost at a rate far in excess of replacements. Defeat in the air appeared inevitable.

His Majesty King George VI believed that another National Day of Prayer should be held. It was set for Sunday, 8 September, just eight days after the Battle for Britain had begun. Once again there was an enormous response.

The following day saw the crisis of the Battle for Britain. Douglas Bader put it this way: '15th September was the day that the Battle of Britain was won. The Germans quit before we did and so they lost. It was as simple as that'.

Years later I heard that Air Chief Dowding said at one of the anniversaries of the Battle of Britain:

Britain was not too proud to recognise National Days of Prayer
and should not be too proud to acknowledge the result of those prayers.
I can say with absolute conviction that I can trace the intervention
of God, not only in the Battle of Britain itself, but in the events
which led up to it; and that if it had not been for this intervention,
the battle would have been joined in conditions which,
humanly speaking, would have rendered victory impossible.

Maybe the chance to fly at last

Military clothing was in short supply at that time. For months we remained in our civilian clothes. There was such a tremendous response of young men from all over South Africa to join up, that there was a huge bottleneck. Large numbers slept in tents.

I was found a place in a huge, one-roomed building that had previously been a vehicle workshop. As the bottleneck prevented us from moving on, we were kept busy by 'square bashing' hour in and hour out, day in and day out. It was tedious and aggravating not to be doing something directly for the war effort.

But there was an up side. One day we heard that the Empire Air Training Scheme had come into being. South Africa had been selected as one of the countries where training would take place. We were given the opportunity to remuster. I was elated and remustered as aircrew. Now I had the chance of becoming a pilot! If I failed in that, I would still be able to fly as a navigator, an air gunner or a wireless operator.

BEAUFIGHTER OVER THE BALKANS

We were moved to another nearby camp, called Lyttleton. Here we were housed in suitable, dormitory-style, wooden buildings. Our ground training commenced without delay. I knew I would stand a high chance of being selected for pilot training if I could achieve a high score in my ground exams and pass some other tests. But it was not long before I realised that I was bound to fail: I knew nothing about trigonometry.

I shared my problem with a fellow who was billeted with me and who happened to be a university graduate. He kindly offered to teach me 'trig', and was as good as his word. Somehow or other he 'sussed out' the types of question that would be asked in the exam. For six weekends he stayed in camp to teach me trig. On sitting the exam, I was amazed to find that I knew all the answers. I scored 98 per cent. At the subsequent acceptance interview I was passed for pilot training, and my status was now a 'pupil pilot'.

By this time many Elementary Flying Training Schools (EFTS) had been opened all over the Transvaal; at Baragwaneth, near Johannesburg, and at Benoni farther along the Gold Reef, with others a long way away, such as Witbank, Standerton and Vereeniging.

To my delight I was assigned to No.1 EFTS at Baragwaneth, as by this time I had become very friendly with a family there by the name of van Rij. The father, Frederick van Rij, had emigrated from Holland to South Africa when he was still a lad.

His mother was a very tenacious woman. Once, when things went wrong with her occupancy of a house that had been assigned to her, she went to Pretoria to see the South African President, Paul Kruger, and had tea with him and his wife on the verandah of their house. She got her home!

Incidentally Paul Kruger and his wife ended up having fifty grandchildren. It sounds unbelievable, but large families were needed to populate such a huge country. The black population was also small. Workers for the gold mines, for example, were brought in from countries to the north.

Frederick van Rij married an eighteen-year old white South African girl, who had been born there and had been held captive in one of the British concentration camps during the Boer War. She never spoke of her experiences, but we know now that large numbers of people died, especially children. Her name was Annie de Visser, and she was of Dutch and French Huguenot descent.

They had thirteen children. The younger ones were living at their Johannesburg home in the lovely suburb of Parkview. One of the younger sons had been killed in a mid-air collision when he was in training to become a pilot. Another of the younger sons had preceded me to Baragwaneth to train as a pilot, but was 'washed out' because of airsickness. He became a navigator instead and eventually overcame his airsickness.

CHAPTER 4

Learning to Fly: The Long-Awaited Day

*A*bout fifty of us arrived at Baragwaneth for the beginning of our Elementary Flying Training School course. We knew that only about half of our number would get through it. Our grass airfield was situated on the top of a hill. It overlooked huge gold mine dumps that had, to my surprise, a white, yellowish hue to them. When the strong winter winds blew, a lot of what had been brought up from the bowels of the earth, and then ground to powder in extracting the precious gold, was blown away – to the discomfort of the people living in that area.

We were issued with flying suits, as we would be flying in open-cockpit Tiger Moth biplanes, which were made of wood and covered with fabric. Flying boots and helmets with speaking-tubes were also issued. It was early on a cold winter's morning in June 1941 when I finally began what I had been attempting to achieve for a whole year!

I was shivering with cold and nervousness when we drank coffee served on a large table out in the open air next to our flight offices. It was so cold that any spilt coffee would soon turn to ice. My nervousness had nothing to do with being afraid of flying, but rather a fear that I might not be up to the standard required to be a service pilot.

Out Tiger Moths were always ready for day and night flying. (SAAF Museum)

BEAUFIGHTER OVER THE BALKANS

I listened to a long preflight briefing by the flying instructor assigned to us. Then I had to strap on the parachute issued to me. I walked alongside my instructor to a yellow-painted Tiger Moth. It was parked on the grass, close to the flying instruction building. There was a long row of Tiger Moths all lined up and ready for the new intake of pupil pilots. Farther on was a huge hangar, where other Tiger Moths were being serviced by SAAF ground crew.

When we reached our plane, it was the first time I had ever been close to any aircraft, let alone flown in one. Planes were few and far between in those days. On our farm in the Great Karoo it was a rare occurrence – very rare – to see a plane flying overhead.

Before we both climbed into our cockpits, the instructor showed me how to do a preflight inspection of this little single-engined plane. It was awkward to climb into the very small and cramped cockpit with a cumbersome parachute strapped to your body. Once that was done, the parachute pack fitted perfectly into the specially designed pilot's seat and had been so efficiently fitted to my body that I sat comfortably on it.

After strapping ourselves in with full shoulder harnesses, and plugging the leads from our flying helmets into the hearing-tube, my instructor, speaking into the speaking-tube, asked in a loud voice whether I could hear him. With that confirmed, he began introducing me to the flying controls of rudder pedals, 'joy stick' for the elevators and ailerons, as well as the gauges on the instrument panel.

Meanwhile an air mechanic was standing by to swing the propeller to start the engine and then to take away the chocks, which were always in place when the aircraft was parked. With switches on, a thumbs-up sign was given, and the mechanic gave the prop a hefty swing.

Nothing happened at first. It took a few swings before the engine burst into life. Seconds later we were taxiing out. I was told to keep my left hand on the throttle, my right hand upon the stick and my feet lightly on the rudder pedals.

In the air at last

As we began to move, I felt exhilarated. Now my chance had come! A few minutes later, with the engine at full power, our wheels left the ground and we were in the air.

I was airborne for the first time in my life. It was very exciting as we climbed. We could look at the nearby mine dumps and the city of Johannesburg in the distance. We turned to fly over a wide valley. The wind was blowing hard, and down below I saw the dry tumbleweed being blown over the African veld. Tumbleweed grows like a ball, growing to about three times the size of a football. It then becomes completely dry, hard to the touch and very light. When the strong winter winds blow, it eventually breaks away and is blown all over the flat ground. It was quite a sight to see from the air.

But I had more important work to do than be taken up with blowing tumbleweeds. I was concentrating hard on everything my flying instructor told and showed me. It was a familiarising

Flying instructors were always identified by their white overalls. (SAAF Museum)

flight. By the time this initial forty-minute flight was nearing its end, I had learned a lot and got a feel of the flying controls.

However, when we came in to land and finally touched down with a perfect three-point landing, with both wheels and tail-skid touching the ground at the same moment, I felt that was beyond my capabilities. I was despondent. I was so short, only 5 ft 4 in (1.6 m), and I could not see out well enough. But, my instructor solved the problem. He said he would provide me with a special cushion about five inches deep, which I could place on the seat under my parachute pack. Next time we flew, that cushion made all the difference. I soon began to feel more confident about take-offs and landings.

Fear sets in!

All was going well on my EFTS course. I was really enjoying flying – until I began to be taught 'stalling'. At full throttle my instructor raised the nose of the plane very sharply and I lost sight of the ground. All I could see was sky. I felt unnerved at losing all sight of the ground. Then, quite suddenly, the aircraft began to judder. As we lost flying speed, the aircraft stalled. The nose dropped sharply and we were nose-diving straight down to earth. I didn't like that either, but worse was to come!

My instructor told me he was going to teach me about 'spins'. Again we reached the stall position. Then, just as the stall began and seconds before the nose suddenly dropped, he kicked the right rudder hard and fully. We were then spinning hard to the right. The ground below appeared to be going round. Then, with the throttle pulled right back and the engine idling, he said, 'Now to get out of a spin, kick hard with left rudder!' Quite quickly the fast spin slowed down. Just as the spinning stopped he centralised the rudders. Once again all was fine. He eased the stick into the neutral position and we were once again flying straight and level. As soon as I began doing stalling and spinning myself, I became more confident and less apprehensive. But it was something I never came to really enjoy!

First solo flight

The day that I had dreamed of came after I had ten flying hours to my credit on the EFTS course. On landing, my instructor said, 'Taxi in, I'll see if I can find another instructor to check you out for going solo.' I dropped him off close to our flying office and kept the engine running. A few minutes later another instructor whom I had not seen before came out. He clambered into his cockpit and, a man of few words, just said, 'Taxi out, Stevens for take-off. Do a circuit and landing.' I did as instructed and made a reasonably good landing.

'Okay,' he said, 'taxi back and drop me off. You can go solo.' I was elated, but somewhat apprehensive, when I found myself all alone in an aircraft for the first time. I was still not very confident about making good three-point landings. I tended to be too heavy on the stick. When

The Tiger Moth was an ideal trainer – not too easy to fly and to make a perfect three-point landing required a fair amount of skill. (SAAF Museum)

coming within a few feet of the ground, I would also pull back on the stick too much instead of slowly inching my plane closer and closer to the ground. As a consequence the plane would 'balloon up' a few feet and then stall, resulting in a heavy landing. However, all went well on this and subsequent solo flights.

Whirlwind disaster

One day, when I was almost at the end of my EFTS course and quite confident that I would not be 'washed out', I came in to land after an hour of upper-air flying. This type of flying involves stalling, spins, looping the loop and 'precision altitude flying' – in other words keeping my plane at exactly the same altitude, even in bumpy flying conditions. I was just about to touch down and was very confident that I was going to make a perfect three-point landing, when suddenly my plane was thrown onto its port (left) wing, then onto its nose and over onto its back.

The impact was violent enough for my head and body to be jerked so far forward that, despite the restraint of my safety harness, my head hit the compass, which was situated right in front of me but quite low down. My helmet saved me from serious injury, but the strain on my body affected my back.

When I carefully unclasped my safety harness and fell onto the ground almost head first, I realised that something was possibly seriously wrong with my back. As I got up and looked at that wreck of a plane, I was aghast at what I had done and could not understand what had happened.

Suddenly I saw a staff car in its war-camouflaged colours racing out over the grass airfield. It

Sometimes we used a large grass field as an auxiliary airfield with a rest tent. At midday it was too hot to be inside.

ground to a stop near me and out stepped the CO and the Chief Instructor. I expected them to be glowering at me for wrecking one of the planes, but instead I seemed to detect unexpected faint smiles on their faces. They asked if I was all right. I hesitated for a moment, thinking that if I told them about my back the Medical Officer might take me off flying. So I said, 'I'm okay, sir.'

Then they told me that I had been hit from my blind side by a small whirlwind that had raced across the airfield. They told me that those in the control tower watched it all happen but were helpless to inform me, as those were the days long before radio-telephony. All they had were large, hand-held Aldis lamps. They would flash a green light at us for take-off and a red light to hold us up. But with that whirlwind there was nothing they could have done to alert me to the danger.

That night, as I went to bed, the pain in my forehead had almost disappeared, but my back was very sore. I felt sure that I had damaged my spine. It was hard to get to sleep, but with a soft pad of a jersey pushed against my stomach, the pain eased. From then on I had to make very sure that I kept my spine as straight as possible.

Washed out: will I be next?

By this time many familiar faces of those on our EFTS course had disappeared. They had been 'washed out' for one reason or another. It seemed to us that they were simply 'spirited away' back to Lyttleton immediately after being given this unwelcome verdict. No doubt it was done to spare them from having to admit to the others on the course what had happened to them, and maybe to protect the rest of us from thinking 'Perhaps I'll be the next'.

Among those who were 'washed out' was the wonderful fellow who had got me to where I was by all his hard work in teaching me 'trig'. I never got to say goodbye to him, and I never saw him again. I assume that he, and all the others who were returned to Lyttleton, would have been offered the opportunity of becoming navigators, because they had all done so well in their ground exams. We heard through the grapevine that one or two of them had opted for training as air gunners. Years later I tried to find this great chap who had helped shape my destiny. His name was Axelrod, a most unusual name. But I could never track him down to once again express my appreciation to him. Maybe he did not survive the war.

My expectation of being able to spend some weekends with the van Rij family, who lived so close by in Johannesburg, did not work out. I had to study hard. It was hard going for me with my very limited education. Many of the others were university graduates. They seemed to take it all in their stride. But for me it was a hard grind, so I missed out on female company. I missed meeting up with the five unmarried van Rij girls, who were still living in their Parkview home with their mother.

At the end of our course we were informed that most of us, if not all of us, were to be sent to the Advanced Flying Training School (AFTS) at Kimberley. We would get our coveted pilot's wings if we got through the course there. We understood that having passed our EFTS course, it was more than likely that we would get through the final course. We would at long last accomplish our ambitions of becoming pilots in the South African Air Force.

CHAPTER 5

Winning my Wings

Kimberley was a famous diamond-mining town. It had a huge, vertical, diamond-filled tunnel that had been emptied to search through the sandy soil to find the minutest of diamonds.

When we arrived at Kimberley for the start of our course at the AFTS, we were shown the planes we would be flying. They looked to us like huge, oversized Tiger Moths. These planes were either Hawker Harts or Hawker Hinds, the two being virtually identical. The casual observer would not have been able to see any difference between them. They were single-engined biplanes with two open cockpits, and were of a wooden, fabric-covered construction.

They were, indeed, very old. The RAF no longer wanted them. South Africa was so short of suitable training planes that they had accepted them. Nevertheless it was always with a sense of awe that I would climb onto the wing and settle into my cockpit. Two mechanics, one on each wing, would start winding away with a crank handle. Eventually the engines would start with a roar. I soon began to love the power of those engines.

Flying our very old Hawker Harts and Hinds over Kimberley's thorn tree-studded veld. (SAAF Museum)

Salt pan landings

Out in the African veld of the Cape Province, hundreds of miles to the south of Johannesburg, were a number of dry salt pans. We used them to practise 'forced landings' during this AFTS course. We would fly high above the salt pans and throttle back our engines, just keeping enough power to prevent our engines from stopping. Then we glided down and landed without power on one or another of these small but ideal landing grounds.

It was not as easy as it may sound. One had to get one's plane into exactly the right position and height for the approach. It was better to be slightly too high than too low. If one was too low, one had failed, and engine power would have had to be used to prevent disaster. But if one was a little too high, it was possible in those planes to sideslip away those extra feet. But that was not the ideal. To execute a perfect forced landing, everything had to be right.

Occasionally I would see a landed plane on the ground below me, with the pilot standing next to it. I knew then that his engine had stopped. He could not, of course, start it himself. All he could do was to hope that one of us flying above his particular salt pan would fly back to our air base to alert the mechanics of the problem. Two of them would then make their way to him by air or truck.

What I enjoyed most was dropping small flour-bombs on the bombing range. We would let them go at almost zero feet. I loved that. Such low flying was exciting. Just next to the target spot a high wooden tower had been built. One of our fellow pupil pilots would be on observation duty when we were dropping our bombs. It would be his duty to write down the number on our plane, the time of the drop and how close the bombs were to the target when they exploded.

Dicing with death

At the far end of that target run there was a row of huge eucalyptus trees, which we always called simply gum trees, because of the gum that exuded from the bark. Sometimes it would appear on the trunk of the tree crystal-clear and tempting to eat. I tried it once or twice. It was not particularly palatable to my taste buds. One day, after I had released all my bombs, dropping only one bomb on each run, it struck me that it would be fun to fly as low as I could and see how close I could get to those trees before having to pull up vertically. From then on I did this at the end of every run, gradually getting closer and closer with experience. But I could never be quite sure how close I was getting to them. I could no longer see the trees when I yanked back on the control column because the raised nose obliterated my view.

I decided there was only one way of finding out if I was getting as close as possible: flying to the limit, as it were. I had to get so close that my wheels would brush the leaves and small branches at the top of the trees. With practice I became very successful. I felt that I had mastered the art. As I look back now, I think I must have been mad. I did not have the experience to calculate either the wind conditions or the change of performance of individual planes, or the loss of performance of these old planes on very hot days.

Then one day, when I knew that a friend of mine, by the name of Gray, was in the observation tower, I thought I'd give him a fright. So I did the same with that tower. Later that day, when we met up with each other, he told me that he was petrified. He was sure his end had come. The word spread among the others. I started to hear that they were predicting I would be the first of that course to be killed. They knew that foolhardy pilots did not survive for long.

Nevertheless I did survive that foolishness. Nor did it stop there. And yet I survived. It seems on reflection that I had a charmed life. I took so many chances over the years and escaped the gunfire that was thrown up at me from all sizes of anti-aircraft guns. I am convinced now that it was because my father and stepmother prayed for my safety every day.

The racehorse that bolted

When my father was with the British Army of Occupation in Germany, after the end of the First World War, we were billeted in a large house. There were stables for a number of horses. My father owned and rode a couple of racehorses. He bought 'Capitas' for £9. On it he won many races. He also had a polo pony.

An officer friend also kept his polo pony there. One day they went for a ride through a large forest. My mother decided to accompany them and rode one of the racehorses. During a gallop through the forest, her horse bolted and she could not rein him in. Then, suddenly, in front of them a small horse-drawn cart began crossing their path. That did not stop the excited racehorse: he kept going and attempted to jump this cart at full galloping stride. My mother was thrown off and received a severe injury to her head. She was rushed to hospital where she received stitches. I was five at the time.

It is possible that this injury to her head resulted in a tumour appearing many years later. I was fourteen years old when she died of the brain tumour. A few years later my father married one of the Scottish missionary nurses that had nursed my mother during her dying days. It was through these fine missionaries that my father, mother and I had become Christians shortly before my mother's death.

Featureless veld

My flying in the AFTS seemed to be going well. And so it should: I think I had the finest flying instructor at the school. He was an older man and a very dedicated instructor. Some of the others had been fighter pilots in Abyssinia or North Africa, and all they wanted was to get back into the fight once more. But Capt Stark was not like that. He was absolutely committed to train his pupil pilots to the very best of his ability. So I had every chance of being turned out as a competent pilot.

One day Capt Stark sent me off solo on a triangular, two-hour, cross-country flight. I studied the map and could find very few landmarks: only one train line and very few roads. Before take-off I set my compass for my first course. Turning onto course, I climbed up to a few thousand feet above the ground. As I flew across the level and open African veld, I began to feel very uneasy at not being able to recognise, or rather find, any landmarks. They just didn't exist. I was solely reliant on my compass.

I had noted the strength of a cross-wind and had adjusted my compass accordingly. I was soon far away from the town of Kimberley and was beginning to feel lost. When I was within a few minutes of my estimated time of arrival at my first turning point, I was beginning to feel very nervous and distrustful of my compass. I was looking anxiously ahead, looking first to one side of the large engine in front of me and then to the other. But I could see no sign of the few houses that should be there.

As panic set in, I began to scan the whole countryside to my left, looking as far as I could, and then to the right. I was beginning to feel completely lost. Then suddenly, right in front of me, I caught sight of those few houses that had blended into the veld so well that they were not easily discernible. I breathed a sigh of relief. From then on I never again doubted my compass. I took the second leg much more confidently. The last leg was very easy, as I was returning to the large town of Kimberley.

It was my ground exams that had me worried. It would be terrible if I passed all my flying tests and then failed to win my pilot's wings by failing my ground exams. I knew how bright and well educated those were who had been with me at Baragwaneth, and I was sure that those who joined our course from some of the other Elementary Flying Training Schools were equally bright as many of them were university graduates. So once again I had to keep my nose to the grindstone. My social life had to be kept to the minimum.

Temptation Resisted

On Sundays I rested. I went to church in the morning and was always asked home by one family or another for lunch to spend the rest of the day with them. One family was very hospitable. The father was quite a few years older than me. He had a young, attractive wife and a little daughter. One evening he went away to preach and left me alone with his wife and their young child.

When it became dark, the moon rose over the horizon in its full glory. It was a full moon. The air was crystal-clear. The moon was so very clear and large that it completely dominated the sky and lit up brightly everything that was within my gaze. While the little girl was being put to bed, I was on the verandah (or 'stoep', as we would say in South Africa), sitting rather precariously on the banisters of the railings, with my feet up and my back resting on one of the uprights. I was drinking in the beauty of the night.

BEAUFIGHTER OVER THE BALKANS

There was silence: no sounds of cars, music or voices. All was still, apart from the sound of the crickets, which also seemed to be enjoying the wonders of the night. Occasionally a bat would swoop, snatching a flying insect on the wing. It was in that wonderful and, what seemed to me a romantic, setting, that I suddenly realised that my friend's wife was standing close to me. As we drank in the night air scented faintly by one of those large, flowering shrubs that somehow gave off more of its delicate scent by night than by day, it was a night of romantic appeal.

As this lovely young lady stood very close to me in her light, cotton summer dress, I was very tempted to slip my arm around her waist and to draw her close to me. I had the feeling that it would not be unwelcome. But I resisted the urge and the moment passed. Later, when reflecting on that moment of temptation, I was so glad that I had not succumbed and betrayed the trust that my friend had placed in me when leaving me alone for the evening with his attractive young wife.

What a cheek!

I became twenty-one that year on 27 August. To my joy and great surprise I received a congratulatory telegram from one of the five van Rij girls: from Kathleen, known by some as Kath, but by most of us as Kay. She was one of the youngest of that large family and a very attractive young lady.

I had once tried to kiss her in their kitchen, but she resisted me. Then one Saturday we drove many miles out of Johannesburg to spend a day picnicking at some falls and bathing in the crystal-clear pool. I climbed one of the steep, rocky hills surrounding the pool with Kay and some others. We sat on a huge rocky slab, looking down on those immediately below us who were having fun in the pool. I sat myself down next to Kay, and a few minutes later I slipped my arm around her waist. She thought I was very cheeky and resisted me!

Mid-air collision avoided

When our ground exams were over, I waited anxiously for the results. I did not think I had failed, and I should not have done so after all my hard work. But one cannot easily tell when the various exams covered so many subjects. It was a relief to eventually hear that I had passed them all. I had not done very well or very badly. My score was about half-way down the list of around eighty pupil pilot students on the AFTS course. It was not until the very end of the course that my grades in flying would be recorded in my pilot's log-book. I was rated as 'average', and once or twice as 'above average'.

I had one more flying test to take: my final test as a service pilot. I was shattered when I found that my flying ability was to be assessed by our Commanding Officer, Lt Col Pope. I should add that in those days the South African Air Force used army ranks. I was rather frightened of my CO. He was not much taller than I but I thought him rather distant and gruff. And so I felt very nervous when I climbed into the cockpit.

I flew with him for nearly an hour and he put me through everything in the book. Finally he said, 'Okay, Stevens, go back and land.' I was determined to make a perfect three-point landing: touching down on both wheels and tail-wheel at the same moment, so smoothly that not even the slightest bump could be felt. It was never easy, but especially not when one was nervous because it was a test. I flew back to our grass airfield and joined the flow of other Hawker Harts and Hinds to make what we called a square circuit: keeping at the right height of 1,000 ft (300 m) and not too close to the airfield. One had to be very exact in one's flying.

I was on the last leg, getting myself, or rather my aircraft, into exactly the right position before throttling back and turning onto my final approach. With my eyes firmly fixed on the airfield, judging when to make my final 90° turn, I suddenly felt that I should look up – but why? As I did so, I could not believe my eyes: another aircraft was immediately above us, only a few feet away. We were about to have a mid-air collision any second.

I immediately put my plane into a dive to my left and shouted out to my CO. He had not seen the danger at all. When I regained my composure a few seconds later, I found that I was by now too close to the airfield to make a normal approach. I was in quandary: should I start all over again by doing the square circuit all over again? Or could I dare to sideslip off all that extra height and then straighten out at the last minute? If I did that, I knew it would be almost impossible to make a perfect three-point landing.

With those thoughts rushing through my mind, I decided to risk the second option. I immediately dropped my left wing until it was almost facing the ground. I kicked hard with my right rudder. Then I raised the nose to drop off speed right down to landing speed. The wind beat hard against our left cheeks as we lost height quickly and dramatically. As the rapidly approaching ground came up to meet us, I was concentrating hard, ready to pull out of that sideslip at the last minute.

When that moment came, when we were only about 50 ft (15 m) above the ground, I had to move fast to get my plane back onto an even keel. I also had to make sure that I kept the air speed absolutely right. I had to be immediately ready to put down this rather cumbersome plane on its three wheels simultaneously and as softly as possible. It all happened so fast. One second we were in the air, then next safely on the ground. We landed so smoothly that we could hardly feel it! I was elated.

My CO. could not believe it. He knew that no pilot, however experienced, could have done better than that. For it to be done by a rather inexperienced pupil pilot amazed him. It was, of course, a fluke: or was it an answer to the prayer of 'Oh God – please help me!'? Either way, Lt Col Pope was impressed. He gave me such high marks that the final marks for flying and ground exams added together made me come out top of my AFTS course of nearly 100 fellows.

Years later, after the war, he was once again my CO. I was then a staff instructor at Central

BEAUFIGHTER OVER THE BALKANS

Flying School at Dunnottar, near Springs at the far end of the Gold Reef in the Transvaal. One day in the officers' mess, as we talked together, he said, 'You are the only pilot to whom I ever awarded an exceptional rating.' I gulped. I did not tell him that when Capt Stark filled in my final assessment form, he only rated my flying ability as average. And he should have known. He had flown dual with me many times and had been my flying instructor throughout the AFTS course.

Fighter pilot hopes dashed

But there was a sting in the tail of being registered as coming top of the AFTS course: I had lost my chance of becoming a fighter pilot. More than anything I wanted to become a Spitfire pilot. When our postings were listed on the notice board, I found that all those who had come near the top of the course had been creamed off to become – flying instructors!

I was very annoyed. One of the fellows was a few years older than the rest of us, and he was married. In my opinion it would have been more appropriate to select *him* for flying instruction, rather than a foolhardy pilot like me. He would surely have been eminently more suitable for such a job than I. But there was nothing I could do about it.

Pilot's wings at last

A few days later a great and very moving event took place: the 'Passing-Out Parade'. Parents and others had been sent invitations to attend the ceremony and the pinning-on of our pilot's wings onto our chests. What made it so special was that one of the South African Air Force bands would be there playing deeply moving music. My father and stepmother, accompanied by our close friend Joe Radford, drove up a couple of hundred miles from Cradock for the occasion. Mr Radford was one of the leading lights in the Cradock Baptist church. He was the youth leader, and we young people appreciated him very much. As we were marched towards the podium, I tried to detect those who had come to be with me when, at last, I would arrive at the place where I had 'won my wings'. With the stirring music being played, we lined up. One after another, as our names were called out, we went forward to receive from Lt Col Pope those coveted pilot's wings.

CHAPTER 6

Flying Instruction: Hazards

Bloemfontein

A few days later we were on the move again. For me and those also selected to become flying instructors this meant that we were on our way to the SAAF Central Flying School. At the time it was situated just outside Bloemfontein, the capital of the Orange Free State. It was with a rather heavy heart and much disappointment that I started this new course. I decided to do my best, even though I was not at all keen on becoming a flying instructor.

My flying instructor, Capt Hauptfleish, was a great chap. He had been a SAAF fighter pilot and was being given a rest from the dangers of war on a temporary basis, before going off again on another tour of duty on combat operations. To do well now was a great challenge to me. All the others were very able, young, newly qualified pilots, who had done well in flying and ground subjects. I should not have been among them. I was only there because of that fluke. Or was it a miracle? Perhaps this was the route God had ordained for me, a part of the destiny for my life.

My flying training, and learning the 'patter' that I would use when teaching pupil pilots to fly, went well. But the ground school lectures were something different. As I sat in class I found that I was often out of my depth. I assumed that all the others understood what was being taught and that it was only me who was not taking it all in. One day I plucked up courage and spoke up, feeling a fool as I did so. To my surprise I found I was not the only one by any means who was struggling. Had I not plucked up courage and been willing to make a fool of myself, then I suppose we would have all soldiered on in the dark, hoping that all would become plain later on. I had wrongly assumed that all the others were much brighter than I, and understood everything the lecturers were teaching.

It was a good lesson. From then on and all throughout my life, I have been much freer in asking the questions that others were too frightened to ask, for fear of being thought of as fools.

When the results of the course came out, I only came sixth. But I was delighted to have done so well against such stiff competition. When our postings were announced, I was disappointed that I had not been posted to Baragwaneth, where I would be close to my Johannesburg friends. On the other hand, though, I was relieved that I had not been posted to Witbank, which was a long, long way away from Johannesburg. My posting was to an Elementary Flying Training

School situated very close to the Gold Reef town of Benoni. This was within easy reach of my friends.

I had bought a car after realising that I would be serving in South Africa as a flying instructor for a year or so. Very few of us had cars in those days. I found a super Chevrolet and bought it for £120, a lot of money in those days. But the car was worth it because it was comparatively new. From then on life began to become even more enjoyable. I attended the Baptist church. For a time I went out with the minister's fine and very capable daughter. But it was a bit of a mismatch: she was very tall and I was very short. There were other differences, too, so it seemed better to go our separate ways. Later she married an outstanding RAF pilot.

On arrival at Benoni in my newly acquired car, I found that the layout of the camp was very similar to the one at Baragwaneth. Some of the first pupil pilots were members of the RAF. One of them, Geoffrey Diamond, was my one and only pupil that had corrective lenses fitted to his flying goggles. He was also the one and only pupil pilot trained by me with whom I kept in periodic touch, up to his death a few years ago. I am still in touch, from time to time, with his widow. She is today confined to a wheelchair, following a mountain accident years ago: she had a nasty fall when she and Geoffrey were climbing Mount Snowdon.

A famous South African pilot
My new CO was Major Allister Miller, one of South Africa's most famous pilots. I did not realise at the time just how famous he was. I only came to realise it when Peter Bagshawe, who has written two outstanding books about South African pilots, wrote *Passion for Flight,* a large-format book containing many photos, in which my story was told as one of fourteen South African airmen. All have since died, leaving me as the sole survivor. Miller's name cropped up in this book time and time again.

Allister Miller was not only very famous in his own right, but he also played a major part in the lives and flying careers of many other South African pilots, who were often called 'Allister Miller's boys'. In the First World War Allister Miller served with the Royal Flying Corps (RFC). He earned the DSO (Distinguished Service Order) for strafing an enemy position, distracting enemy attention sufficiently to allow the cavalry to reach their objective.

He was asked by the RFC to help in recruiting South African airmen. His tours were very successful: 8,000 applied, of whom 2,000 were selected for pilot training. Most qualified as pilots. In 1919, for his work for the RFC, the RAF and the British Government, he was awarded the OBE (Order of the British Empire). During these recruiting tours of South Africa in those early days of 1917, he landed his BE2C in areas where aircraft had not been previously seen. On 7 December of that year he landed on Port Elizabeth's Fairview Golf Course.

In 1929, the year in which I arrived in South Africa as a boy of ten, he founded South Africa's first air service. He named it 'Union Airways', which was eventually taken over by the government and became 'South African Airways', which is today a famous airline. As I look back, I wish we had known all this about him. This famous yet unassuming man became my CO in the early days of 1942.

Edwin Swales VC DFC

One of the SAAF pupil pilots that came to us for his elementary flying training on Tiger Moths was Edwin Swales. He became the only South African in the Second World War to win the Victoria Cross, Britain's highest military award for valour.

He only flew with me once, when I took him on a long cross-country flying exercise, so I didn't get to know him well. He was a big, ruggedly built man who had played Rugby for Natal, and was an all-round sportsman.

By the time he came to us in 1942 he was already a war veteran. He had been in the thick of the Second World War as a sergeant major in the South African Army fighting the Italians in Abyssinia, as Ethiopia was then called, and he had fought the Nazis in the North African campaign.

After that he was permitted to transfer to the South African Air Force for aircrew training. I knew nothing of his background at that time. On completing his elementary flying training with us, he was sent to Kimberley for advanced flying training on the recently acquired twin-engined Airspeed Oxfords, which at that time I hadn't even seen.

Edwin Swales VC DFC

After winning his pilot wings at Kimberley, he jumped at the opportunity of being seconded to the Royal Air Force. With fifty other volunteers he sailed to England, where he joined a crack Pathfinder squadron. He soon became a highly respected and competent leader. After fearlessly and successfully leading many attacks over Europe, he was awarded the Distinguished Flying Cross.

In the closing months of the war in Europe, he was attacked one night by a Messerschmitt night-fighter over Pforzheim, and the Lancaster's starboard inner engine was hit. It also holed the wing fuel tanks and shattered the rear gun turret. Despite all this, Swales continued flying to his target, although by now he himself was a sitting target. Another night-fighter appeared. Its cannon shells put out a port engine this time, and raked the fuselage of the Lancaster along its entire length.

The huge bomber faltered under this fresh onslaught and fell to 4,000 ft (1,200 m) while Swales struggled to gain control. He was just able to circuit Pforzheim and pass on instructions over his radio to the other bombers under his command. Only when he was convinced that the object of the raid had been accomplished, did he turn to the problem of attempting to get his almost unflyable Lancaster back all those miles to base. That night over 1,500 tons of bombs had been dropped. It was one of the most concentrated attacks ever flown by RAF Bomber Command. For the loss of twelve bombers, some 350 acres of a built-up area of Pfozheim had been completely gutted.

For Swales and his crew the journey home was a flying nightmare. In the dark he desperately needed his blind-flying instruments and his artificial horizon, but they had been shot away. He struggled to keep his wallowing bomber in the air. Then they flew into turbulent cumulus clouds. His rudders became uncontrollable and the remaining two engines began to overheat. By this time they were down to 3,000 ft (900 m). An overstrained control cable snapped and the Lancaster began to go into a spin.

Swales gave the order for his crew to abandon the aircraft, which he had expertly flown to Allied-occupied territory. Just after the last member of his crew baled out, he lost control. He had left it too late to bale out himself. The bomber crashed into some unseen high-tension cables and there was a tremendous explosion that lit up the night sky.

At first light, Swale's crew inspected the wreckage of their Lancaster, which was strewn across two fields at Chappelle-aux-Bois on the outskirts of Valenciennes. In the twisted metal ruin of the cockpit, they found the body of their skipper, Ted Swales. His strong hands were still grasping the control column, while some yards away a booted foot still rested in a rudder-bar stirrup.

Determined to give his crew every chance of survival, Swales had remained at the controls until it was too late for him to save himself. His selfless sacrifice was fittingly recognised by awarding him the posthumous Victoria Cross, gazetted on 24 April 1945. Part of his citation read, '...he did his duty to the last, giving his life that his comrades might live'. Captain Edwin Swales VC DFC SAAF was the only member of the South African Air Force ever to receive this supreme award.

Another famous South African, who joined us as a flying instructor, was Bobby Lock. Years before in Johannesburg, when I was sixteen years old, as my father and I were going for a walk in the hot African sun on Parkview Golf Course, we saw a crowd of spectators making their way to the last hole. We hurried to see what was taking place. We got there just in time to see Bobby Lock, at nineteen years of age, win his first South African Golf Open Championship. At the EFTS in Benoni we never saw much of him in the officers' mess. He was always out playing golf in his spare time, and everyone just wanted to play golf with him.

It was not long before I began to get bored with the same old routine of teaching these young fellows to fly. I lacked the dedication of Capt Stark. One day, to my surprise, he turned up at Benoni. Maybe he, too, had got tired of instructing on Hawker Harts and Hinds at an Advanced Flying Training School and wanted a change, although I could not really believe that. I found it far more exciting to fly those larger old planes than the very small Tiger Moths.

Trying an outside loop

One day my attraction to foolhardiness reared its ugly head again. I decided to attempt the impossible: an outside loop. During an ordinary loop one is pressed down into one's seat and the blood is drained from one's head. If it is a very tight loop, one can momentarily suffer from 'black-out', when the eyes lose their vision. But with an outside loop the pressure on one's body is reversed and one is only held in the cockpit by the shoulder harness. I thought about this for a long time before I tried it.

When the moment came, I commenced in the normal way, diving down very steeply to gain maximum flying speed and then pulling very hard on my flying control stick. Then at the top of the loop, when I was upside down in relation to the earth, I executed a half roll and was the wrong side up once more. At that moment I pushed hard with all my might and as quickly as possible. The nose dropped vertically.

1942. When I was a reckless flying instructor on Tiger Moths at Benoni.

However, that was not all I wanted. I struggled hard to do an outside loop, but as the speed mounted up, I knew I would never make it. I simply had to abandon my attempt before this wooden plane broke up in the air. I should have reported what I had attempted to the engineering officer. He could then have had that Tiger Moth checked out thoroughly, to ensure that I had not damaged it by executing a manoeuvre that it was not designed to perform. But knowing that I would be severely frowned upon for what I had tried, I told no-one. Had that plane broken up later on in mid-air, I would have been devastated, but I did not think of it at that time.

Low flying between gum trees

In our low-flying area there were two very tall gum trees standing very close to each other, with no other trees in sight. One day I heard one of the other flying instructors telling how he had flown through the gap between them in a very steep turn. So the next time I took a pupil pilot on a low-flying training exercise, I flew past those trees, looking at the narrow gap between them. It was quite obvious that they were too close together to get between them in level flight without both wings of the Tiger Moth being torn off. I circled those trees a number of times. I felt sure that if the other pilot had been able to do it in a steep turn, then I should be able to do so, too. I did not say anything to my pupil, who was one of our RAF men. Before the war he had been a Brooklands racing driver. I felt panicky but was not prepared to let my fears beat me. Finally I plucked up courage to execute this very difficult manoeuvre. My pupil told me later that he guessed what I was going to attempt. He thought I had misjudged the width of the gap and that I was going to try and squeeze the plane between those two huge trees with disastrous consequences.

At last, I was ready. I approached the trees sideways on at a short distance from them. Just as I was passing them, I threw my plane into a steep turn. Keeping within inches of the leaves of the one tree, with those leaves almost brushing my face, I got safely through. I had to keep as close as possible to the tree I could see, otherwise my wheels would touch the other tree and that would spell disaster. Once again I had been foolish, and once again I had got away with it. When we landed and walked away together from our plane, my pupil told me that he thought his end had come!

Weekends were free unless one was on Orderly Officer or Station Duty Officer roster. And as that did not occur that frequently, it meant that I could drive into Johannesburg and spend that time with hospitable friends. One family, who were closer to me than the van Rijs and where I spent many wonderful weekends, were the Irvings. Their son Jimmie had just joined the SAAF with hopes of becoming a pilot. They also had two teenage daughters: Elaine, still a school girl, and Beth, who had just started work as a secretary. On Saturdays we would fill my car and go out to enjoy ourselves at some lovely place, like Germiston Lake. Often others would join us in their cars.

On Saturday evenings we would all meet up in the centre of Johannesburg at the YWCA. In their large hall we would meet to listen to Gavin Mowat, a missionary from Scotland. He and his wife were working in one of the remotest parts of Africa, in the most northern part of Zambia, which was then known as Northern Rhodesia, named after that famous pioneer, Cecil Rhodes. The Mowats were on a period of prolonged leave. As they were so popular, that hall was filled with young people from different churches every Saturday night.

Nearly hit by an express train

One very late Sunday night on my return to Benoni, when it was very dark, I suddenly saw a black man step into the road waving his red-glassed lantern at me. This was a signal for me to stop, as there was a train approaching. In those days this was our only warning about trains crossing that road.

I looked to the left and to the right for the bright light on the front of the engine, which I felt certain I would see if a train was coming. But seeing nothing, I thought this African man was being too conscientious. Instead of stopping, I pressed my foot down hard on my accelerator and ignored his warning. A second later my conscience made me jam on the brakes hard, feeling that it was wrong to ignore his warning. As my car ground to a halt, to my amazement an express train raced by.

I found out later that I had not seen its light because it had been blocked out by a row of trees. My God-given conscience, which I obeyed, saved my life. It was a close shave. I can well imagine what would have happened if I had been killed. That poor African would most probably have been blamed for falling asleep on duty and for failing to wave his red light at me.

In due course I heard that Jimmie Irving had passed his Empire Air Training Scheme (EATS) ground exams and that he had been selected for pilot training. On hearing this, it struck me that I might be able to arrange for him to be sent to Benoni and that I might be able to train him to fly. I asked him if he would like this. He thought that it was a great idea. So I made application, not really holding out much hope that it would be granted. But it was, and Jimmie became my pupil pilot.

By this time I was becoming very tough on my pupils. I had found that one's mental agility was poorer in the air than it was on the ground. So I developed the habit of shouting out to them in our flight offices: 'What would you do if...?' I would go through all sorts of possibilities, and if they could not, without a moment's hesitation, call back the answers, I would refuse to take them up until they had well and truly got all the answers off pat. When Jimmie came, this is what I was like. It is one thing to have a friendship, it is another to have an instructor–pupil relationship, and it is hard to keep both in balance.

Jimmie did fine and duly passed. He moved on to an Advanced Flying Training School and got his pilot's wings. Then later on he was posted to a Spitfire squadron. He had got what I had wanted so badly! After he left Benoni I wondered if I had strained our friendship by my habit of being so tough on my pupils, but when he got married to 'Cookie' Tomlinson, he asked me to be his groomsman. Yet still that feeling lingered.

It was not until many years later, when we met up again and talked of those days together at Benoni, that I realised that my concerns about the tough way in which I had treated him had not spoilt our friendship. On the contrary, he spoke of me in glowing terms and told me that I was a natural born leader. I knew that I did not deserve such praise, but nevertheless it set my mind at rest once and for all.

The Miracle of El Alamein

It was just before Jimmie Irving arrived at Benoni to begin his flying with me that we heard the disastrous news that Tobruk had fallen. Many South Africans had been taken prisoner, among them the sons of farming families from our part of the Great Karoo. The Germans broke through our defences and took Tobruk. The Eighth Army were in full flight and it was again a time of extreme crisis.

On 29 June 1942 they retreated to El Alamein as a line of defence. When General Rommel arrived the next day, the German radio boasted that Rommel and the Afrika Corps would sleep in Alexandria that Saturday night. It was only sixty-five miles (105 km) away. To all our Allied leaders, it appeared that our North African forces were facing defeat.

Two days after that retreat, the King and Queen, the Archbishop of Canterbury, several members of the War Cabinet, other ministers and ambassadors were present in Westminster Abbey in their official capacity. Special prayers were said was made for all those fighting in North Africa.

Suddenly the advance of the Afrika Corps ceased and the Panzer divisions rolled back westwards. Why? It was a mystery. Rommel later wrote in his 'Papers': 'Our strength failed in front of El Alamein.'

Although we knew very little about all that was happening in 1942, it later transpired that Rommel had become ill for the first time in his life at that time, and General Stumme had taken his place. However, the day after his appointment he died of a heart attack.

On 3 September, Westminster Abbey was crowded to capacity for that second National Day of Prayer of the Second World War. The King and Queen, other members of the Royal family, and Members of Parliament were present. Despite it being a weekday, people flocked to churches all over Britain to pray.

When General Montgomery took command he declared: 'The soldiers must have faith in God.' Not only was Alamein held, but within three months Montgomery was ready to launch the Battle of Alamein offensive. It began at 9.40 on 23 October. He issued to the Eighth Army this Order of the Day: 'LET US PRAY THAT THE LORD, MIGHTY IN BATTLE, WILL GIVE US THE VICTORY.'

By the time Rommel arrived back in North Africa on 25 October, the battle was already lost. As his General Cramer said: 'Alamein was lost before it was fought. We didn't have the petrol.'

Eight days after the opening of the Battle of Alamein, Churchill addressed more than three thousand miners, saying:

'I have a feeling sometimes that some Guiding
Hand has interfered. I have a feeling that we
have a Guardian, because we have a great
Cause, and we shall have that Guardian so
long as we serve that Cause faithfully.
And what a cause it is.'

Long afterwards Churchill said: 'Before Alamein we never had a victory. After Alamein we never had a defeat.'

It has been said that the South African Air Force pilot Don Tilley (who was later to become my CO in Italy), did more than any other man to win the North African campaign, by sinking the fuel tanker that was bringing fresh supplies of urgently needed petrol to Rommel and his Afrika Corps.

The great concert

During my time at Benoni we were entertained from time to time by concerts that were put on for us in local halls. One group that came our way was a cast of entirely black young people. I think it was the best by far of all those who came to Benoni. The lead lady was talented and beautiful and I found her very attractive. This was in those unfortunate days when there was not much in common between blacks and whites. After the show, I would have loved to have gone round to the back of the hall to meet them and say how much my colleagues and I had appreciated the show they had put on for us. And I would have liked to have met up with that young lady!

I had become a Christian at the age of fourteen through the influence of some missionaries to the Zulus, just before the death of my mother when we were farming in Natal. I was baptised in a river with a number of Zulu men and women and had attended a number of Zulu services at Murchison Mission Hospital. I suppose, however, that more than anything else, the language barrier prevented me from getting closer to any black people.

Low-flying 'beat-up' fright

That Easter I joined all those from our Saturday-night class in the Johannesburg YWCA at their Easter camp at Henley-on-Klip. That camp helped to cement our friendships, as did those meetings and our often going together to a large cafe afterwards in the centre of Johannesburg on those Saturday nights. 'Klip', the Afrikaans word for 'stones', was the name of a very stony river. Henley was a holiday resort with a hotel, where we had some of our meals.

Across the river from the hotel was a grass field. It was on the edge of this lovely river, with its huge weeping-willow trees growing close to the water's edge. On that field many white bell tents were erected for our accommodation. We had a great weekend that Easter. On the Sunday we climbed into our rowing boats, and in a line each boat followed the leader, rowing up and down the river singing well-known Easter hymns. Our efforts seemed to be well received by the other visitors to Henley-on-Klip.

I had to return in my car to camp on Sunday night to be ready for flying on the Monday morning. That Monday was a Bank Holiday for all my friends, and driving home that night I hit on a plan. Perhaps I could arrange to take one of my pupil pilots on a blind-flying cross-country the next day, and arrange for Henley-on-Klip to be our first turning point. It happened to be about the right distance from Benoni for that purpose.

Early on Monday morning I told my flight commander the exercise and route I had worked out to take one of my pupils on. As it was to be a blind-flying exercise, he would be flying on instruments and would have a cover over his head so that he could not look out. All that mattered was that I could recognise the turning points. He had to call out to me from under his hood when he thought we were flying over a turning point. I would then confirm it to him or otherwise. He

South African young people's church group from Johannesburg at their annual Easter weekend camp on the banks of the Klip River, 50 miles south of the Gold Reef in 1942 at Henley.

A SA Army serviceman on leave. Five years after this shot was taken I married Kay van Rij, the second girl from the left.

On the Sunday we went on the river in a string of rowing boats tied together to sing Easter hymns to the other campers.

would then reset his compass and turn onto the new direction for the second leg. And so it was that my poor, unsuspecting pupil took off blind.

After making a satisfactory blind take-off, he climbed our under-powered Tiger Moth to the required height. This took a long time in a plane with such a small, low-powered engine. Meanwhile I was planning what I intended to do, in my foolhardiness, when we got to Henley-on-Klip. When we arrived overhead, my pupil called out that we should be there and that he was turning onto the new course. I said to his great surprise, 'Note the time, and release your hood cover clip. I am going to take over for a few minutes. You can watch as I do a "beat up" of this camp where I spent the weekend and where my friends are camping. But when you get back I want you to forget about what you are about to see and tell nobody.'

With that I throttled back and dived down onto the camp, intending to give them all the fright of their lives. All those around their tents looked up when they saw me diving at them. Those in their tents came rushing out to see what was happening.

51

On the Monday Bank Holiday I was back on my flying instructor duties. On the turning point at Henley I took over control to visit my friends.

I heard a click when I passed over this car. One of my Tiger Moth's wheels had bent its radio aerial. Amazingly I never noticed that another aircraft from a nearby SAAF EFTS flying school was watching me. He might easily have reported me.

Coming down to scare my friends.

Our camp leader, Mr Voke, an older man, lay prostrate. On seeing these photos I felt ashamed of my reckless flying.

BEAUFIGHTER OVER THE BALKANS

I approached the people, tents and the few cars that were there so low that the wheels of my plane were almost scraping the ground. I flew as close as I dared, before yanking back on my control stick and zooming over them. In my excitement I got carried away, and when I flew over one of the cars, I heard a distinct click. I wondered what it was but soon dismissed it from my mind. Then I saw some of my friends in rowing boats on this wide river and decided to frighten them too, by coming up behind them. But although most of their view of what was happening was obscured by huge willow trees, they must have known exactly what was taking place. So when I started to creep up on them from behind, with my wheels almost touching the water, they were disappointingly not surprised at all.

Having done that, I was ready to climb up over those high trees and drop down on the other side of them to do one last 'beat up'. I was then going to climb away and get back up to the required height to hand the plane back to my nervous pupil. He would then fly blind once more on the new course, on the second leg of his three-leg triangular cross-country exercise. With my adrenalin running high, my brain was no longer functioning in a calculating way. When I turned towards those high trees, I completely forgot to consider if my plane had enough power in its engine for me to pull back hard on my stick and soar over those trees. It was one thing to do that in those powerful Hawker Harts and Hinds, but it was a different ball game in a Tiger Moth.

At the last moment I yanked back on the stick. All was well for the first second or two. Then suddenly the airspeed dropped. The flying controls became sluggish. I suddenly felt a deep anxiety. As we almost reached the top of a tree I began to feel that ominous juddering which is the tell-tale sign that the plane is about to stall and crash. For a second I felt all was lost and that a crash was inevitable. The wheels seemed to almost clip the uppermost leaves, and then we were over, still juddering. In front of us were those white tents and my friends looking up at us. I began to feel that we were about to crash into those tents and kill some of my friends, and probably my poor, innocent pupil, too. Then, to my great relief, as I lowered the nose slightly, pointing directly at those tents, my plane gained just a little speed. The juddering died away, and at last we were able to skim over those tents and fly away!

My heart was beating madly as we climbed away. My foolish behaviour that morning at Henley-on-Klip has left me with mixed feelings: on the one hand, thankfulness to God for sparing me, the life of my pupil and the lives of my friends; on the other hand, anxious thoughts of how that foolhardiness almost led to disaster and death. The thoughts of that day have kept coming back to me disturbingly, time and time again over the many, many years that have passed since that day.

I ended with a 'beat up' of my friends on the River Klip. My adrenalin was running high and I forgot how underpowered my Tiger Moth was at this altitude of nearly 6,000 feet above sea level. I felt an ominous juddering of a stall as my wheels brushed through the leaves. It was a miracle that I did not crash and kill some of my friends.

The next Saturday, I was back in Johannesburg again and at our meeting. After the meeting I found that Russell Clark, a keen photographer, who had been at the camp, had a set of enlargements on display on large trestle tables. What I saw on all those photos of my 'beat-up' shook me. It is one thing acting in the heat of the moment; it is another thing to see it before yourself in black and white. Then one of my friends came up to me and said casually, 'You bent the aerial of my car with one of your wheels'. So that was the click I had heard. What I saw sobered me even more and riveted the memory of that day indelibly into my mind, as photos so often do.

'Dog-fight' disaster

One would have thought that such foolish behaviour would put an end to such things for good and all – but no. Some time later, after one course of pupils was coming to an end and they had passed their ground exams and flying tests, one of my fellow instructors said to the three of us who were with him: 'Let's meet over the low-flying area and have a "dog fight".' We all agreed to meet at such and such a height and time. We laid down no rules, not even which way we would turn away if we met head on!

BEAUFIGHTER OVER THE BALKANS

Of the four of us, one was my best friend, Basil Lamb. He was a devout Catholic, and his older brother was a priest. He and I had a lot in common. We did not drink or tell smutty jokes. Basil was a great soccer player. The previous Saturday he had scored the winning goal for his team at their match in Johannesburg at the famous Wanderers playing field.

We met as agreed. It was exhilarating but highly dangerous. I am surprised that it did not result in a mid-air collision. But it did end in disaster, though not in the way we could have expected. It so happened that Basil was attacked more than the rest of us. In his under-powered plane he lost height and flying speed and crashed. I saw it all happen.

I saw Basil's pupil climb out and try to help Basil. Fearing that the plane might catch fire, I impetuously throttled back to land next to him. I did not even take a look at where I was to land. Just a few seconds before touchdown I saw an inconspicuous water well in front of us. Mercifully we just got over it before the plane stalled, and we landed safely. As the plane ran along the ground, I unzipped my parachute harness and jumped out before my plane had stopped rolling. My pupil joined me as we ran towards the crash. By the time we arrived, Basil's pupil had pulled Basil clear. He had a broken back. In due course an ambulance arrived to take him away. I then checked carefully my selected take-off path and flew back to base.

That was the end of the flying career of all four of us for some time to come. We were immediately grounded pending an enquiry and assigned to non-flying duties. We were banished to other flying schools. I was sent to the EFTS at Witbank, a coal-mining town miles and miles away from Johannesburg.

A romance had sprung up during those many months at Benoni between Beth Irving and myself. It was almost inevitable, because we were together in her parents' home for so many weekends. She was a lovely girl and I was very fond of her. I thought we were very suited to each other and that one day we would marry. But I did not pop the question. I was only just twenty-two and she was barely eighteen. The war was on and the casualties were terrifically high.

I expected that sooner or later I would be released from my flying instruction duties and be sent 'up North', as we used to say. I might be shot down and killed. If we married, Beth would be left as a young widow. And what if she was pregnant at such a time? Nor did I feel I was ready at such a young age to settle down to the responsibilities of married life.

Beth evidently felt she was ready for marriage. When she began to feel that our relationship was not going anywhere, she one day told me that she was thinking of someone else. This coincided with the time of my being sent away to Witbank, so we drifted apart. Many months later I heard that she had become engaged to a fine, tall, good-looking man. He was also a devout Christian, who, even at that time, was a preacher. Later he became a well-known speaker and a good Bible teacher. He also headed up the fine work of 'Youth for Christ'. His name was

The wreckage of the Tiger Moth we 'shot down'! Unfortunately my friend and fellow flying instructor, Basil Lamb, broke his back in this incident.

Dennis Clark, the younger brother of the man who took those photos. Years later Beth and Dennis moved to Worthing, England, and had four children. I, too, married and had four children, but we lived in London.

One day my wife and I went down to Worthing to spend a day with them. That afternoon we decided to go to the seaside. As Beth and Dennis did not have a car and ours was only small, it was decided that Beth and I would go by car to take all eight of our little children with us, and that Dennis and Kay would catch a bus. Beth was heavily pregnant with their fifth child at that

57

time. When we arrived at the seaside and clambered out of our little car, I do not think those who saw us could believe their eyes: a blonde couple, with eight children, who were also all blonde except for one of them, and a ninth on the way.

Now Dennis has long since died, but Beth is still in Worthing. And through her we came to live in Worthing, too: so in our old age we are neighbours!

As a punishment for our 'dog-fighting' episode, we were grounded for six long months. I did not like that. Nor did I like being sent away into exile to such a far-away place as Witbank. Nor did I like my duties: I was put in the control tower. It seemed ironic that I could watch all those Tiger Moths but was not allowed to fly in them. The months dragged.

One day, when the WAAFS challenged the officers to a game of hockey, I, who had never played hockey before, became part of the team. It turned out to be a frightening experience. Those girls were big and tough and rough. My shinbones felt as if they had been permanently damaged by the time the game was over! Of course they well and truly thrashed us!

Because we were so far away from anywhere, we had a cinema on the camp and saw some great films. Among those that I will never forget was *The Wizard of Oz*. Although I saw it all those years ago, my memory of it seems to still be crystal clear.

CHAPTER 7

Pietersburg

Flying twin-engined Oxfords

$\mathcal{E}$ventually, after what seemed to be an eternity, my days of being grounded at Witbank came to an end. I was delighted to hear that I had been posted to Dunnottar. I was assigned to a conversion course on twin-engined, low-wing Airspeed Oxfords.

When I first saw this plane and climbed into it I was delighted. No longer would I be sitting rather uncomfortably cramped in an open cockpit, having to shout down my speaking tube to my pupils. Now I would be in a closed cockpit, with my pupil sitting next to me. I would be able to speak to him in a loud voice, but no longer would I have to shout. I could observe his every movement and all his reactions. No longer would our vision be impaired by an engine in front of us. This open forward, unobstructed vision was a delight, something I had never before experienced. I also found Oxfords easy to fly.

It was a pleasure to instruct on the Airspeed Oxford and within an enclosed cockpit. Flying was safer with two engines and the visibility was excellent. (SAAF Museum)

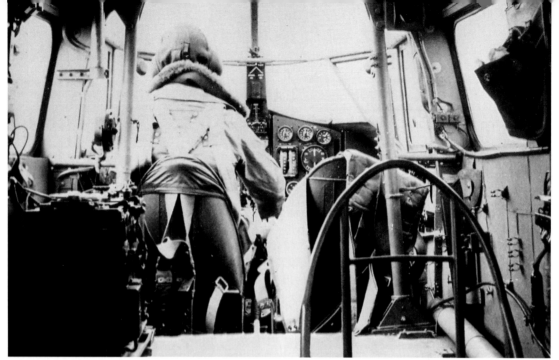
In Oxfords I did not have to shout at my pupil and I could also watch him. Another pupil could also sit behind us to observe all we were doing. (SAAF Museum)

As by now I was quite an experienced flying instructor, I sailed through that course without any problems. At the end of it I found that I was being posted to Pietersburg in the Northern Transvaal. Again I would be miles and miles from Johannesburg. But this time I did not mind. I would be flying again, and flying a fine plane. No longer would I be anxious about an engine failure. Now I had the extra safety of two engines.

But not everything went as smoothly as expected. When it came to night-flying, I found that this was not done on our main Pietersburg grass airfield but on another large airfield some miles away. When night fell it was unbelievably dark. The only lights we could see were the gooseneck paraffin lamp flares marking both sides of our take-off and landing path at intervals.

When I took off with one of my pupil pilots next to me, the last of the flares suddenly disappeared under the wings and I could no longer see the ground. Nor could I see the horizon in this dark sky. My eyes were glued on to my blind-flying instruments. I was by now an experienced instrument flying pilot. Nevertheless it is one thing to fly on instruments under a hood, with another pilot in the plane with you to keep a lookout for other aircraft and see out to be sure that you are doing everything right. It is a very different matter when you are flying on instruments in such darkness.

I had never experienced such darkness. At Baragwaneth, when I was flying at night in the vicinity of our airfield, there was rarely a moment when I could not see the lights from the Gold Reef towns. It had been the same at Benoni. At Kimberley and Bloemfontein our airfields were so close to the towns that we were hardly ever away from seeing the lights on the ground below us.

I could not wait to make a climbing turn to my left, until, once again, my pupil pilot, on looking out, told me that he could see the lights of the flares below me. I felt much happier after that. I did not fly too far away from those comforting flares.

Because we had no radio and no radar in those days, we had to be very careful to avoid mid-air collisions. Our planes had wing-tip lights. I remember one dark night when a new moon gave us enough light to see the horizon. I was sure that we were going to be involved in a mid-air collision with another plane. I was convinced it was approaching us. I called to my pupil pilot, telling him of the danger, and took evasive action. But later I had my doubts. I think I was taking evasive action from a very bright star that I had mistaken for the wing light of one of our Oxfords.

Our auxiliary airfield was not only used at night but also by day, to avoid too much congestion of so many planes taking off and landing all day long. So sometimes we would be flying from the main airfield and at other times from the other one. Because this one was so close to the designated low-flying area, which was almost completely uninhabited, we always planned to teach our pupils low flying from that airfield. It was poor veld country for farming, and in our large low-flying area there was only one white farmer's homestead.

It took us quite a time to teach our pupil pilots how to fly in close formation. (SAAF Museum)

Inset – After an hour or two of loose formation flying they gradually gained confidence. (SAAF Museum)

Our Airspeed Oxfords over the Transvaal on 16 February 1944.

Dating Eva from the air

One day, as I flew over our low-flying area, I noticed that the corrugated iron roof of a homestead had three large letters scrawled on one side: EVA. I assumed that Eva must be a young girl, the farmer's daughter. I began making a point of flying over that homestead once every day that I was flying in that area. I did it many times, but there was no sight of Eva. Perhaps she was a schoolgirl away at boarding school, or maybe at college in Pretoria or Johannesburg. Then, one day, there she was, standing next to their house, looking up as I flew overhead. I decided to have a closer look at who I assumed was Eva.

I flew very low and as slowly as possible. I opened a little side window and stuck out my hand to wave at her. She waved back. When I landed and had a cup of coffee before taking off again with another pupil, I struck on an idea and wrote on a scrap of paper: 'Will you come out with me? If so, lift up both your arms.' I wrapped that piece of paper in a clean handkerchief to take with me on my next flight.

When the time came and I flew towards the homestead, this young lady appeared once again. I had in my hand the note tied in my handkerchief. I took careful aim, and, with my arm once again out of the window, I judged when to let it go as accurately as I could. Hoping that I had succeeded in dropping it accurately, and that she had seen it and recovered it, I flew in a circle and once again began my approach. She was standing there with both arms held high. We waved again and I was gone. That night in my room at our air base I pondered what I had done, wondering how I would make any further contact with this attractive young lady.

Then, a few days later, the commandant of the WAAF, an older lady, approached me and asked, 'Are you Steve Stevens'? She then asked, 'Is this your handkerchief?' It had been washed and ironed and neatly folded. I felt somewhat embarrassed. She then said, 'Eva and her parents would like you to have dinner with them at the hotel this coming Saturday and go with them to the cinema afterwards.'

I felt very awkward when I arrived at the hotel and made myself known, but they were warm and friendly, and I soon felt relaxed with them. We had a great evening together. This led to them inviting me to visit their farm and to spend the next weekend with them. But Eva's holiday soon came to an end, and she was off again. By the time she returned home again, I had gone 'up North' and we lost touch.

Years later I was based at Waterkloof air base outside Pretoria on a short course. One day when I was having lunch in the officers' mess, an army officer approached me. 'Are you Stevens?' he asked. Then, to my surprise, he said, 'My wife would like to see you.' He led me to where they were staying, not telling me who his wife was. When the door opened, it was Eva. I do not know how she found out that I was there. I was glad to see her again and to find that she had married a fine fellow.

The 'flat spin' that killed three

One day, when I was high up in the sky with one of my pupils, miles away from our air base, I just happened to be looking down at the veld below us when I saw a crashed plane. I dived down to investigate. I could see no sign of life. It was one of our Oxfords. To my surprise it had not broken up very much and was not scattered over a large area. I had to assume that the pilot and his pupil pilot were either lying severely wounded in the plane or dead. I flew back to base.

On landing I taxied right up close to the Chief Instructor's office, climbed out and ran to his office to tell him what I had found. An ambulance was dispatched for a long, uncomfortable ride across that open veld. A plane also took off to find the crashed plane, with the information of its whereabouts that I had provided. It would direct the ambulance to the crash. Not only did they find that the pilot and his pupil pilot had been killed, but another pupil pilot had also been killed. Occasionally we would take one of our other pupils with us on certain instruction flights. He would stand behind our seats to learn all he could from observation. It worked well and saved time, because he could hear all I would be saying and he would be able to see all that was going on. The crash must have happened because the flying instructor was teaching spins but got into a flat spin without being able to get out of it. They must have crashed in a flat attitude. Those were the only fatalities at Pietersburg during all the time I was there.

One Saturday afternoon I really made a fool of myself. Another officer and I had been out together. On our way back to base, we were thirsty and called in at a café. We sat at a table for four in this large café. At another table not too far away, I noticed a very attractive lady sitting with an older lady, who I assumed to be her mother. It so happened that we were facing each other, and I kept looking at her. She obviously noticed my gaze. As we left the café I wondered who she was. A few days later I got wind that word had spread among the officers' wives, who were living in Pietersburg, that that fellow Stevens had been 'making eyes' at the CO's wife!

I was aghast. So that was who she was. But how did she identify me? I suppose she must have asked who that very fair-headed and very short pilot was. No doubt she had told her husband, Kalfie Martin, a big bull of a man, and a great rugby player in his day. I had always been in awe of him. Feeling very embarrassed, I hardly showed my face in the officers' mess after that. No longer did I congregate with the other officers to play snooker. I slipped in to have my meals and slipped out again. I did not want to be seen by my CO, who sometimes appeared in the officers' mess. None of the other officers ragged me about this incident. Either they had not heard or were being very discreet. I was glad that I never bumped into the CO's wife again. I thought I had perhaps affronted her. Or was she just mildly amused? I'll never know.

We had some unusual fellows among our pupil pilots at Pietersburg. One of them, who flew with me from time to time, was a Polish officer still in his Polish officer's uniform. He had seen something of the horrors of war, but his English was not good enough for us to be able to find out much about him.

One of our other pupils was a European prince. He was treated the same as everybody else and just known as Alexander. One day I was taking him up on a blind-flying cross-country exercise. It did not go well at all. His take-off was fine, and he climbed away on instruments well, but as he turned on to the first leg of this cross-country flight, he was flying in the opposite direction. I looked down at the compass. He had set it correctly, but the needle was pointing 180 degrees in the wrong direction. He was flying a reciprocal course! I did not want to fail him there and then, so I tried to give him some hints, but nothing worked. He even seemed to be somewhat aggravated by my remarks. Perhaps as a prince he was not used to that kind of approach. Finally I told him that he was flying a reciprocal course. He proceeded to argue with me. That was enough: I shouted at him to let back his blind-flying hood and look out to see for himself. He was shattered. That subdued him a bit!

Preparing to bale out

Another of my pupils was a massive RAF man, who had been a policeman. I found him to be rather clumsy, and I wondered if he would ever make it and be up to standard. One day we were high up in the sky and a long way from either of our airfields. I was teaching him the art of throwing a plane into a sudden steep turn. It was a very important manoeuvre to master, because if ever it had to be done when flying very low, it would be so easy to allow the nose to drop and crash into the ground. To execute a steep turn effectively and accurately, four controls had to be coordinated simultaneously: the throttle, the ailerons, the elevators and the rudder. I asked him to keep his large feet gently on the rudders and to note carefully how I used them.

I also instructed him to keep one hand on the throttle, to see how much more power from the engines was needed in a steep turn. The other hand was to remain on the control column, to feel how much I would have to pull back as I dropped a wing to commence the steep turn. At the same time his eyes must be on the horizon to see that the nose of his aircraft was not dropping. He also needed to watch where he was going. I knew it was not easy, but these able pupils always learnt very quickly.

But not this one! I showed him; he then tried and failed. I showed him again, and he again tried and failed. This went on and on. I became aggravated and short-tempered. I shouted at him that I was taking over *once* again. This time I threw the twin-engined Oxford into yet another steep turn. I yanked back on the control column with all my strength, when suddenly I heard a crack and the plane began to judder. I hastily came out of the steep turn, but the juddering did not cease. I was very worried and wondered if this plane was about to break up. I immediately turned to fly back to our main airfield, as we were losing height fast. I soon began to feel that whatever power setting I used on the engines, and whatever speed I used, there was nothing I could do to hold our altitude. I doubted whether we would make it back to base.

Down below, the African veld was covered with numerous anthills, which are almost as hard as rock. There was just nowhere to get down safely. I began to feel that there was no alternative but to bale out! I told my pupil to unstrap himself, climb back over his seat, clip on his parachute pack and go to the door to be ready to jump. I had always *wanted* to do a parachute drop. Now I *needed* to do one! But instead of being excited at the prospect, I found that I was distinctly nervous. I just did not want to bale out. So I tried once more to see if I could keep this plane flying. I found that if I reduced revs on my right engine, and flew on maximum power on my left engine, I could reduce the rate of descent. But to keep from stalling, I had to fly twenty to thirty miles an hour (32–48 km/h) faster than normal stalling speed. I felt that we might just make it back to base and that we should give it a try. All I could hope for would be to come straight in, no matter which way the wind was blowing.

As we approached the airfield, I saw that all the other planes were taking off and landing at right angles to my line of approach. This would be very dangerous. I might collide with a plane taking off or one of those landing. I hoped that those watching out in the control tower would notice that we were in trouble. They might realise that we were coming in to land so dangerously that they would flash their red light from their Aldis lamps at all incoming and taking-off aircraft. It was touch and go. We skimmed over the fence at high speed. I brought the crippled plane down to within a foot of the ground and cut the engines. It dropped that final foot or so like a stone. We breathed our sighs of relief.

No one in the control tower had seen our coming, which was not surprising. They did not expect to see any plane attempting to land from that direction. Fortunately we landed so close to the fence that no other planes were put at risk. I stopped the engines. We climbed out to see if we could find out what was wrong. We were surprised to find that the cowling under the right engine had come loose and was acting as an air brake. I was amazed that what I considered a small matter could have such a dire effect upon flying this plane.

This poem expresses what I was feeling at the time.

The Flying Instructor's Lament

What did you do in the war Daddy?
How did you help us to win?
Circuits and bumps and turns laddie,
and how to get out of a spin.

Woe! and alack! and misery me!
I trundle around in the sky,
And, instead of machine-gunning Nazis,
I'm teaching young hopefuls to fly;
Thus is my service rewarded,
my years of experience paid,
never a Hun have I followed right down,
nor ever gone out on a raid.

They don't even let us go crazy,
we have to be safe and sedate;
so it's nix on inverted approaches,
they stir up the CFI's hate.
For it's oh such a naughty example,
and what will the AOC think?
and we never get posted to fighters,
we just get a spell on the link.

So it's circuits and bumps from morn till noon,
and instrument flying till tea,
'hold her off, give her bank, put your undercart down,
you're slipping you're skidding' that's me!
And as soon as you're finished with one course,
like a flash up another one bobs,
and there's four more to show round the cockpit,
and four more to try out the knobs.

But sometimes we read in the papers
the deeds our old pupils have done,
and we're proud to have seen their beginnings,
and shown them the way to the sun;
so if you'll find the money and turn out the planes,
we'll give all we know to the men,
till they cluster the sky with their triumphs,
and burn out the beast from his den.

The Miracle of Malta

By now I was becoming more and more frustrated that I had not been allowed to go on 'active service' in the war zones. We knew that Allied landings in Europe would soon take place. Victory was still a long way off, but it was in sight. Miracle after miracle had continued to occur after each of those National Days of Prayer. They were very apparent to Army, Naval and Air Force leaders.

One of the miracles of those days was Malta. Why didn't Malta fall? The Italians could easily have taken it. So could the Germans. Had Malta fallen – which was so strategic – we might well have lost the Second World War. The island was virtually unarmed, having only sixteen anti-aircraft guns and four Fleet Air Arm Gloster Gladiators.

General Dobbie, whom I met years later after the war, in his and Lady Dobbie's flat in London, had been appointed Governor of Malta. In a special Order of the Day, he said: 'It may be that hard times lay ahead of us, but however hard they may be, I know that the courage and determination of all ranks will not falter, and that with GOD'S HELP, we will maintain the security of this fortress.'

General Ironside sent General Dobbie a personal telegram containing a Bible reference, Deuteronomy 3:22. Looking up the text, General Dobbie read: 'You shall not fear them, for the Lord your God, he shall fight for us.'

Hitler gave permission for a surprise attack on Malta – Operation Hercules. It was twice put off and finally postponed 'until after the conquest of Egypt', which never happened.

Not only was Malta held, but from this tiny island the Allied forces harassed enemy shipping. Don Tilley, who was just one of many South African Air Force airmen who were at Malta by this time, had done so well that he had been awarded the Distinguished Flying Cross twice.

Later Sir William Dobbie wrote *A Very Present Help – the story of the siege of Malta from 1940–42*. It is full of illustrations of God's help and interventions. In it he wrote:

> *God's restraining hand continued to be strong for us for a period...*
> *We were very conscious of God's protecting hand, constantly*
> *evident in many ways. We saw it when He restrained the enemy from*
> *invading us at a time when we were ill–prepared to resist. We saw it in*
> *the results achieved by our pitiably weak air defences... It is a miracle*
> *which cannot be gainsaid. It is God who works such miracles.*

Preaching in lion country

During my time of service at Pietersburg it was a great advantage to own a car. Without transport, a social life with local people would have been very restricted. As it was, I linked up with the Methodist Church and got to know quite a few people at church on Sundays and at the mid-week meeting held in the minister's manse. I got to know the minister and his wife quite well. On hearing that I had obtained a diploma at the Bible Institute of South Africa, as well as a letter from the Principal confirming that I was competent in conducting services, the minister asked me if I would be a lay preacher for him in his Pietersburg circuit. It was one of the largest in South Africa, perhaps anywhere: it covered an area of 40,000 square miles (more than 10 million hectares).

John Halifax and SAAF and RAF pupil pilots and flying instructors at our air station at Pietersburg in 1942.

One of my assignments was to conduct and preach at a service in far-away Messina, in the northern-most part of South Africa, close to the Limpopo River and close to the border of Southern Rhodesia, now known as Zimbabwe. It would be a round trip of 400 miles (640 km). I was to drive up to Messina on the Saturday, spend the night with members of the church, take the service the following morning and drive back after lunch, getting back in time to get some sleep on Sunday night, before my flying duties began again on Monday morning.

Fortunately Eva's father had given me extra petrol. He had also replaced one of my tyres, which was wearing out, with one of his old tyres that was in much better shape than that old one of mine. The long drive took me through flat, open veld country, which was largely uninhabited. When I neared Messina, I found it was a place of rocky outcrops. I had been told it was lion country.

Messina was a small town with a large public swimming pool. They did not have a church building. The service would be held at the swimming pool. It was a new experience to me to conduct a Sunday church service with my congregation all sitting in very large deck-chairs all around the swimming pool. The deck-chairs had huge sun canopies fitted to them. It was a very hot day. Although I was only dressed in shirt and shorts, I was perspiring freely! A small, easily portable pedal organ was used to play the hymns. And so from this open-air swimming pool, the praises to our God rang out and were no doubt heard by many in this sleepy little town of Messina. It was a day I will never forget!

That was my only visit to Messina, but I often went down south about seventy miles (110 km) to a place called Potgietersrust. It was also a farming area town but larger than Messina. They had a lovely church building in the middle of the town. I usually took with me an RAF pupil pilot from Southampton, by the name of John Halifax. He was a dedicated Christian. He and I would take the services together. We struck up warm and lasting friendships with two families in particular. John and I became life-long friends. On our way down to Potgietersrust we passed two, almost identical, pointed hills. They were most unusual and very prominent. They were called 'Sheba's Breasts'. The breasts seemed quite an appropriate name, but why Sheba's? I was informed that it was in this part of the Northern Transvaal that Rider Haggard wrote his well-known books *King Solomon's Mines* and *Sheba*.

John at the controls of his No. 30 Squadron RAF Wellington in Italy.

One of the bridges the Wellingtons destroyed in Italy, north of Ferrara on the River Po.

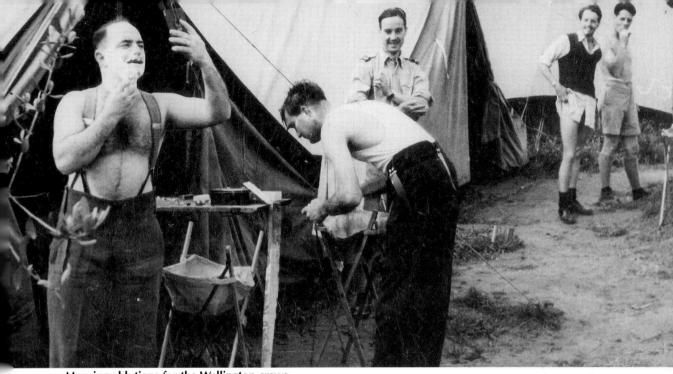

Morning ablutions for the Wellington crews.

John Halifax, who won his pilot wings at Pietersburg, went on to combat missions in Italy flying Wellingtons. He is seen here with a destroyed tank near Veltera.

BEAUFIGHTER OVER THE BALKANS

Sugar Loaf Mountain flying experience

In that area there was a large mountain shaped like a sugar loaf. There were many such shaped mountains in South Africa, but this one was outstanding. The top was absolutely flat, and there were sheer drops of hundreds of feet on each side. I often used Sugar Loaf Mountain to experience one of the most exhilarating flights of my life. I would approach it with my wings almost touching the shrubs growing on this small plateau. Then, roaring across the top, I would suddenly reach the other side. One moment I would have the ground just a few feet below me, the next moment I would feel as though I were being catapulted into the air. The ground, which had been so close, suddenly, and without warning, disappeared. It was a terrific experience.

Passing out in a decompression chamber

In those days we would take up our pupils to, as I recall, around 20,000 ft (6,100 m) for 'altitude tests'. By this we would see if their movements became sluggish at such altitudes, where oxygen was in short supply. Today this would never be allowed, as it is now known that to go up to such

Steam locomotives at Suloma.

heights without oxygen can cause brain damage.

John Halifax in a railway shed at Suloma looking at some steam locomotives bombed by Allied forces.

But I doubt if this was ever allowed after a decompression chamber arrived one day on a lorry. It was offloaded between our flight offices, situated on the edge of our grass airfield and the hangars for our planes behind our offices. A number of us took turns in going into this small metal ball. The others gazed through the small, thick, glass porthole type of window at the particular fellow whose turn it was to sit at a small table with a notebook in front of him and a pencil in his hand. He was asked to write and keep writing for the whole time he was in this decompression chamber. While we were sitting there, the oxygen would be slowly extracted.

As we watched through that porthole, we would begin to detect that he was not coping too well. Then it appeared that he was having difficulty in keeping on writing. Then he dropped his pencil, and a few seconds later his head dropped. At this point the oxygen was pumped back in. As this was done he raised his head and picked up his pencil to begin writing once again. Soon after that he was let out, and someone else went in his place.

Then it was my turn. When I came out, I was ecstatic. I exclaimed triumphantly: 'Well, I didn't pass out!' 'Oh yes, you did!' was the response of those who had been watching me. I was emphatic that this was not so. I was shown my notebook. I could see that my writing continued as normal for a while, then it became barely legible and then there was a break in my writing. Then it began again as a squiggle, before becoming normal once more. That convinced me!

No longer did I have any confidence about going up to 20,000 ft (6,100 m) with one of my pupils. I do not recall whether the arrival of a decompression chamber at Pietersburg changed our procedures or not. I suspect it must have done. But, as I never had cause to take another pupil up on an 'altitude test' after that, before leaving to go 'up North', I do not know what happened.

Answered prayer

Something rather remarkable happened to me after I had been at Pietersburg for some months. I had wished for someone to be with me in the officers' mess who shared my Christian faith, for I had not found anyone among my fellow officers. So I began to pray and ask the Lord to send someone to me. Some time elapsed. Then, one day, I was in the officers' mess ordering a coke at the bar, when I noticed a newly arrived RAF officer drinking a soft drink. I wondered if this might be the fellow I had prayed might be sent to be a suitable close friend to me.

I approached him. His name was John Stokes and he was from Devon. I soon realised he was a very solid Christian and told him that he was an answer to my prayers. He told me that he had been very disappointed in being posted to Pietersburg: he had wanted to be closer to Johannesburg, where he had friends. He said he was now going to write to his wife, Myra, back in England, to tell her why he had been sent to Pietersburg! We struck up a lasting friendship. Years after the war I visited him and met Myra in their lovely Devon cottage. He was teaching Scripture and sport at a local grammar school. He was a strong, heavily built man and a good sportsman. I thought those two subjects were a great combination for a Christian teacher. Unfortunately, he has long since died.

CHAPTER 8

Released at Last for Active Service

$\mathcal{S}$ ome months later, and after a strong friendship had developed between John Stokes, John Halifax and me, the day came when I was quite suddenly informed that I was to be released from my duties as a flying instructor.

I had been teaching young fellows to fly for over two years. Now at long last I hoped I would become a Spitfire pilot. I drove to Pretoria, after saying goodbye to those I had worked with and my Methodist friends in Pietersburg. I stopped on the way at Potgietersburg to say goodbye to the Hudsons and the Watts. They had given John Halifax and me such warm and generous hospitality on our weekend visits when we went down to take their Sunday services.

At Roberts Heights (now called Voortrekkerhoogte) I was accommodated at the SAAF officers' mess, while I was given a medical check and jabs to give me immunity from the various diseases to which I might be exposed in North Africa and Italy. Then the day came when I walked up the steps into a twenty-eight-seater aircraft – a DC-3 that we knew as a Dakota. It was the largest plane I had ever seen.

Our destination was Cairo. It took five days to get there in this slow-flying plane. It was stiflingly hot when we arrived at the Almaza transit camp, close to Cairo. I shared a tent with an old friend, Percy Lindsay Rae from Durban, whom I had not seen since our pupil pilot days. That night when I was in a deep sleep, I felt an animal jump onto my bed. Would it bite my exposed face? I was petrified but I could not rouse myself out of my slumber. Then suddenly it jumped off. Maybe it was only a cat!

Rocket-firing Beaufighters

Next day we went to the SAAF HQ. They took one look at our pilot's logbooks and, seeing how experienced we were as pilots, they announced that we would be sent on a captain's course on four-engined heavy bombers. We remonstrated, telling them in no uncertain terms that we wanted to be fighter pilots, preferably on Spitfires. They almost laughed at us, saying it would be a waste of our flying experience to be put onto fighters and, in any case, we were too old for fighters. We were only twenty-five!

We returned to our tent with heavy hearts. That night we decided that we would return to SAAF HQ the next day to try and persuade them to change our assignment to something more exciting than being a 'taxi-driver'. That was our mistaken view of being the captain of a heavy bomber.

It may have been in one of these Bostons, seen here over Cairo, that my former pupil Geoff Diamond frightened the daylight out of me.

We were excited to be flying Beaufighters but we did not realise its dangers of tailplane instability.

Our Beaufighter Conversion Course at Shalufa in the Canal Zone of Egypt on 4 November 1944. I'm seated on the left with my observer Joc Mitchell behind me wearing a beret.

They listened to us and finally said they would put us on Beaufighters, if we would like that. I had never seen a Beaufighter and knew nothing about them, but liking the name, we eagerly agreed that that would suit us fine. We returned to our camp elated.

While waiting to be posted to an Operational Training Unit (OTU) based at Shalufa, near the Suez Canal, I made contact with my very first pupil pilot, who was now an RAF officer testing Bostons. He invited me to fly with him. He put me into the navigator's seat in the nose of the plane. I had never seen a plane like it and was very impressed with the plane and his capability in flying it.

Then after he had checked it out after its overhaul, he came in to land. I was surprised at his very steep approach. My surprise changed to fear when we were low down and the runway was coming up to meet us so fast. Sitting there in the nose of the plane, I felt we were going to hit the runway nose first and I would be killed. But at the last minute he lifted the nose and made a perfect landing. I was relieved and impressed at my former pupil's ability.

A few days later we arrived at Shalufa and were shown the twin-engined, low-wing Beaufighter. We liked what we saw. I especially liked the wonderful forward visibility from the pilot's seat. But as there was only room for one pilot at a time, we had to fly with a flying instructor in a similar type of plane first. So we were taken up in a Blenheim. They were old, war-weary planes that had

Sixty-four members of No. 19 SAAF Beaufighter Squadron B Flight aircrew and ground crew with one of our Beaus on the sandy Adriatic seashore covered with perforated steel.

Sixty-four members of A Flight. Photos were taken of almost everyone in our squadron around Christmas 1944 when a thaw melted the snow away.

seen better days, but they served their purpose. We were trained in them by our flying instructors to fly our rocket-firing 'Beaus'.

While down in the Canal Zone, I met up again with one of those who attended our Johannesburg Saturday night meetings, or 'classes' as we called them. Syd Hudson-Read was a great tennis player. But as he had not played squash, I taught him. I felt rather devastated when, after only a few games, he beat me!

I met up with many I had known when we first became part of the Empire Flying Training Scheme. We had been scattered all over South Africa at different Flying Training Schools. Now we had been released quite suddenly for combat operations. This was due to the fact that the Empire Flying Training Scheme had become so successful, that we were now training more than enough airmen to replace all those who had been shot down and killed or taken prisoner, and also to meet the needs of new operational squadrons.

When our OTU flying training and our ground instruction was over, we were on our way to Italy. At Bari, where we spent a day or two before moving on, I was surprised to meet Jimmie Irving in the officers' mess, whom I had not seen for a long time. He had just completed his tour of operations on Spitfires and was on his way home. I wanted to hear all about his experiences, but he was not very communicative. Perhaps what he had gone through was more than he could bear to talk about at that time. Now it is too late to ask him. He died quite recently.

Joining the Balkan Air Force

Those of us who were due to join SAAF Beaufighter squadrons were told that some of us would be sent to No.16 SAAF Squadron and others to No.19 SAAF Squadron. These were both based close to the village of Termoli, on the Adriatic Coast. They were close to the river Biferno, half-way up the Eastern side of the leg of Italy.

Those who had been trained to fly four-engined heavy bombers were to join two four-engined Liberator squadrons. We were all to be part of the Balkan Air Force (BAF), which had been formed a few months earlier to operate in direct support of the Partisan forces of the Balkans, especially those of Marshal Tito of Yugoslavia.

During the first four months of the existence of the BAF, 114 ships, 211 locomotives, 643 motor vehicles and 63 enemy aircraft had been destroyed. Despite these losses, the Nazis were holding on tenaciously, but were being continually harassed by Tito's Yugoslav Partisans and the constant air attacks from the various BAF squadrons.

When Yugoslav was invaded in 1941, King Peter and the government fled to London. That, no doubt, cemented a relationship between Britain and Yugoslavia.; but not to the same extent as Britain's relationship with the Poles who fought with us so tenaciously and heroically.

By April 1941 all the major cities of Yugoslavia with its population of sixteen million inhabitants had been subjugated. But because it was such a mountainous country, it was ideal for guerrilla warfare.

Our Nissen hut ops room with a table where we could study our maps before a low-level rocket-firing attack. Hanging from the ceiling were models of enemy aircraft that we might encounter when over the Balkans.

All the information we needed was here. Huge maps of all the Balkans were on the walls and the latest tactical information was on notice boards.

Sgt Robinson and one of his men with a new set of our photos that he has just printed for us to come and see and to study.

Josip Broz, better known as Tito, led the Partisans, resulting in the Germans having to deploy over half a million troops to hold the Balkans. Tito was highly respected by Hitler who said of him:

> To call a man like Tito a Marshal is absolutely correct. A man who has practically
> no material at his disposal, who keeps a keeps a full enemy force constantly
> on the alert, and who always recuperates from our blows deserves this title
> more so than some of our own colonel generals and field marshals who
> could not operate skilfully with the finest machine the world has ever known.

Hitler had attempted to destroy Tito in May 1944, when 750 paratroopers overran Tito's secret headquarters in Drvar. Yet, Tito and his staff were able to escape, taking with them 118 wounded Partisans. A month later General Eisenhower established the Balkan Air Force with Air Vice Marshal William Elliott as its commander to coordinate the planning and execution of trans-Adriatic operations of all three services. It was to establishing an extensive liaison network with Allied land and naval force commanders at Bari and with Tito on the island of Vis.

By this time Tito's Partisans had become a formidable force of 300,000 men. The Partisans, with the formation of the BAF, were able to request us to launch air attacks. For large general targets like railway depots, heavy bombers would be used. For small targets, light bombers would be used, but for small specific targets, such as a building housing a German HQ when the Partisans did not want the rest of the town or village to be destroyed, it was our rocket-firing Beaufighters that would be wanted.

The prime objective of the BAF was to afford maximum assistance to Tito's Partisans, by that time known as the Yugoslav Army of National Liberation (JANL), by providing arms, equipment and air support for its operations against the Germans.

The land and sea forces were to secure a base on the Dalmatian coast so that supplies could be infiltrated by sea. While air operations were crucial, a much greater tonnage could be moved when safe ports were available. Until this was accomplished, combined land and sea forces were combined to carry out attacks against German forces on the Dalmatian islands and coast.

The multi-national air force of the BAF contained twenty-four squadrons of fifteen different types of aircraft and aircrew of eight nationalities – British, American, South African, Polish, Italian, Greek, Russian and Yugoslav – all under the control of the BAF. The main emphasis of this campaign was on air power.

There were a large number of SAAF aircrew at the reception centre at Bari waiting to be sent to the various squadrons, which were all based at various places on the Italian side of the Adriatic coast. Many of us had been involved in the training of aircrew at one or another of the thirty-three South African Empire Air Training Schools, which by this time had trained 16,000 aircrew, including 5,000 pilots, a similar number of observers and 2,000 air gunners, as well as wireless operators and others. Some of those at Bari were going to join Spitfire, Kittyhawk, Mustang and

Our cameraman, Sgt Robinson, in charge of our photographic department, with one of our hand cameras that we sometimes took with us for our observers to use to show the result of our attacks as we sped out of the danger zone for home. In the background is our Nissen hut ops room.

Mosquito squadrons. Not all of them, by any means, were experienced pilots. Many of them had only recently become qualified.

When we arrived at Biferno, we found that Nos 16 and 19 Squadron camps were about a mile from each other. I was sent to No. 19. We did not see much of our other colleagues from then on. Our camp was situated on a hill overlooking the sea. Running close to the seashore we could see our narrow runway. It was constructed of perforated metal that had been rolled out onto the sand.

My fearless observer Joc Mitchell, who had been in the Army in the North African campaign.

Major Don Tilley DFC and bar who later became our CO and won a DSO.

We could also see our Beaufighters in their dispersal bays. They were spread out over a large area, so that in the case of air attacks, as few as possible would be destroyed. But there were not only Beaufighters there. There was another SAAF squadron, which was flying Marauder bombers, and to our surprise, an Italian medium bomber squadron flying Baltimores.

Joc Mitchell, who had recently become qualified as an observer and a wireless operator, teamed up with me. He had served with the South African Army in North Africa and had been in the thick of the fighting. After that he had applied to be transferred to the South African Air Force for aircrew training. We were given a very small tent to sleep in. It was situated in an olive orchard. A corrugated Nissen hut officers' mess was erected in an open space close by. Close to that was a smaller Nissen hut that was our operations unit, where we would receive our briefings before each flight and would also gather for debriefing after each of our rocket-firing attacks of enemy targets in the Balkans.

In the operations unit we were shown the magnificent photos that had been taken. All our Beaufighters had been fitted with wonderful cameras in the noses of our planes, each carrying a long roll of film. As soon as the pilot pressed the cannon button or the rocket button, the camera would start taking photos automatically every second or two, until the film ran out. There was also a tumbler switch that the pilot could switch on himself at any time.

Miraculous Escapes

*W*ithin the first ten days of joining this Beaufighter squadron, Joc Mitchell and I were nearly killed twice! Our first brush with death came about when our CO, Lt Col Don Tilley – a famous pilot who had been awarded the DFC twice – wanted to find out how capable I was as a pilot. At the same time he wanted to check out a newly qualified pilot by the name of Steve Schonveldt.

He wanted to know if we had the abilities to fly in close formation just a few feet above the ground. So we took off on our very narrow, metal runway one after another, in quick succession. I then closed in for tight-formation flying. I wanted him to understand that I was by this time an experienced pilot and could fly in very close formation.

That day I flew in closer formation than ever before in Tiger Moths, Hawker Harts and Hinds or Airspeed Oxfords. I tucked in my right wing between his wing and the tailplane. My right engine was only a foot or so from the back of his left wing. Don Tilley's observer had fear on his face, and with his eyes on the propeller of my right engine, he began to signal to me with his hand to move away. My CO, on the other hand, who had to concentrate on flying his plane so close to the ground, kept turning to look at my plane that was so very close to his. He was not at all fearful and I saw a big smile on his face every time he turned his head to take a look. He was so absorbed with flying so low and glancing round that he was not paying close attention to where we were heading on this large expanse of open, flat countryside.

High-tension cables

Steve Schonveldt, being a very new pilot and not at all experienced at close-formation flying, did not dare come at all close. And this was what saved all our lives! He took his eyes off his leader for a moment, something one is never supposed to do when flying in close formation. To his horror he saw that we were about to fly into high-tension electricity cables. He yelled out over the radio, 'Look out!'

Hearing the anxiety in his voice, I immediately took my eyes off the wing of Don Tilley's Beaufighter and could not

Steve Schonveld to whom I owe my life. He often flew as my No. 2. He took some of the great rocket-firing Beaufighter attack photos.

believe my eyes: there, towering immediately in front of us, were all these cables. Should I try and get under them, with very little room to spare between them and the ground? Or could I get over them?

In a split second I made my choice and pulled back with all my strength on the control column. At the same time I had to slam the throttles forward to full power. The great Beaufighter responded. Its nose rose almost vertically and we all soared over those cables. It had been touch and go. We owed our lives to Steve Schonveldt. My friendship with him became very real from that day on. I had nearly been killed before ever attacking an enemy target.

Our great nose cameras

Although over sixty years have slipped by since my thirty-five rocket and 20 mm cannon air strikes over the Balkans in late 1944 and early 1945, my memories are still vivid. It is due to those wonderful cameras in the noses of our Beaufighters and the magnificent photos we were able to take. When we were attacking a target we were always concentrating so deeply on all factors involved in hitting it exactly at the right spot that there was never a second to spare for 'sightseeing'! My right thumb would be pressing down on the button on my control column to fire

With my great Beaufighter with its wonderful nose camera, Joc Mitchell and some of my ground crew mechanics.

Wherever there were a number of railway trucks there would be many ack-ack guns. Here at the Yugoslav railway siding at Benova Jeruga the guns got Kruger and his observer. We never heard of them again. Puller was hit in one engine, feathered it and got all the way back on one engine.

my four 20 mm cannon. That was easy: I was firing at random, firing for my own protection, hoping to put the fear of death into any unseen ack-ack enemy gunners who were intent on shooting me down.

What required deep concentration was first to find the exact target and – with much difficulty at times – to fly my Beaufighter in a straight line to the target, and at the right angle of attack. Not from too low or too high. Added to that the speed needed to be exactly 220 knots. That would

Van Dyke's Beau was also badly hit at Benova Jeruga. As the Beau was a strongly built aircraft he was able to fly it back. Had it been a Mosquito it would have broken up.

As we headed for home we could still see flames at 50 miles and smoke at 80 miles. Three hours later a Mosquito flying overhead took this photo. The smoke of our attacks was rising to 10,000 feet.

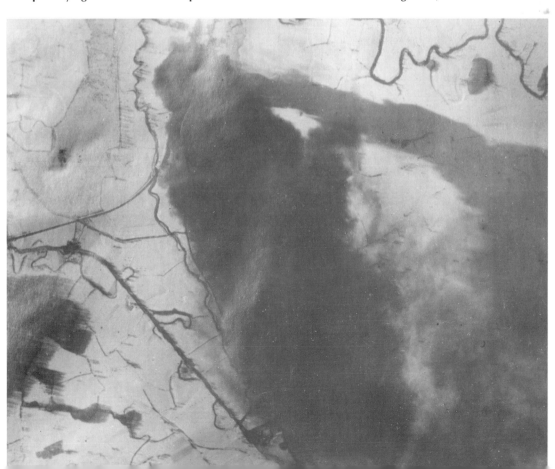

often mean a quick grab of the throttles to increase or reduce power. I really needed an extra arm and hand for that, but had to make do with just two! I needed to have both hands on the control column to fly the plane accurately and to prevent any forward or backward pressure on the control column that would cause a negative or positive 'G'. That would mean that if I should press the rocket-firing button with the slightest 'G' factor, the eight rockets would leave their rails under my wings and follow a slightly curved path to their target. And, of course I also needed to keep my hands on the control all the time because I wanted to keep firing the cannon with a thumb on the button and to be ready at the right second to press the rocket button, when I was at the exactly right distance of a few hundred yards from the target. So there was hardly a moment to look around.

But when that evening we were called into the ops room by our photographic sergeant to see the best of our photos mounted on display panels for us to see, we would say something like 'Oh, I didn't see that, did you?' As I still have those photos my memories are still as vivid as they were sixty years ago. Added to that, Steve Schonveldt who often flew as my No. 2, was, like me, a keen photographer. Most of the other pilots rarely used the camera tumble switch to set their cameras in motion on the run-up to the target as the other Steve and I did. Their photos were taken, without any help from them, by the automatic camera switch devices connected to the cannon and the rocket-firing buttons. This resulted in Steve and myself getting the best photos of our air strikes.

The following are accounts of some of the most memorable of my thirty-five air strikes. They are still very much alive in my memory and come to life in a very real way every time I look at these photos. A decade ago I wrote them up for some of the leading British illustrated aviation monthly magazines. Three appeared in *Flypast* – Britain's top-selling aviation magazine.

Saved by a 12-inch square piece of armoured glass

My next brush with death took place on my very first rocket-firing attack. The Yugoslav Partisans had sent a message to the Balkan Air Force Headquarters, asking us to destroy German-held barracks. It was decided that this was a suitable target for Beaufighters. Eight Beaufighters from our No. 19 Squadron and eight from No.16 would be needed to do the job. It took us nearly two hours to get to the barracks in Bjelovar. As we got close, we were in a mountainous part of Yugoslavia. Low cloud made it very difficult to find our target, and we had to be very careful to avoid mid-air collisions with sixteen aircraft attacking the same small target.

We had expected to all be coming in from the same direction, but in such poor visibility it was not at all straightforward. I only found the barracks when I was almost upon them. When I was very close and firing my four 20 mm cannon, which had set off my camera, and just before I let my eight rockets with their 60 lb warheads go, I heard a sharp crack in front of my face.

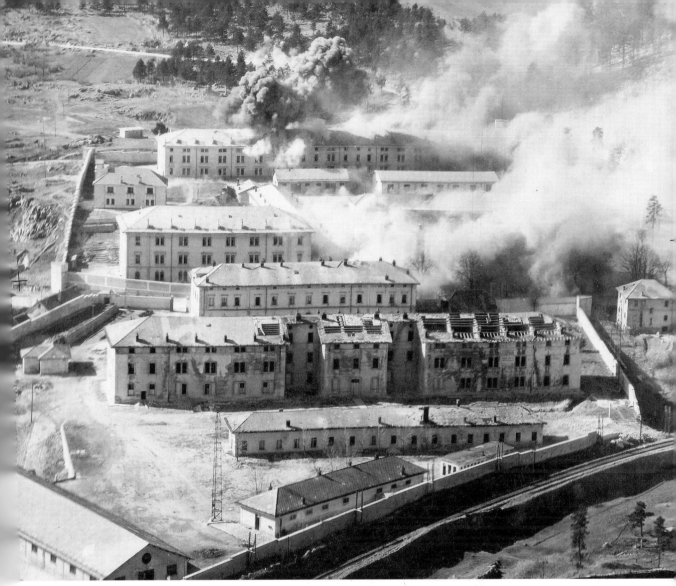

To disrupt the Nazi-occupying forces in Yugoslavia we would attack barracks like this huge one. Taken from Lt Franklin's nose camera just before he fired his rockets.

I had been hit by enemy anti-aircraft gunfire. My head should have been blown off. But I had been protected by a small piece of armoured glass that was a couple of inches thick. It was only about a foot square and situated right in front of my face. It was the only armoured protection in the whole plane.

When I released my rockets a second or two later and flew away out of the danger of those anti-aircraft guns, I took a close look at the damage. The shell had almost pierced its way through the glass, but it held and my life was saved. And so was the life of Joc Mitchell. Had I been killed, our Beaufighter would have crashed into those Bjelovar barracks.

When we got back, we were informed that No. 16 Squadron had lost one aircraft. When the photos from our nose cameras had been printed and were up on display, I could see the high gun-tower situated on one side of the barracks. That must have been the one that was so nearly successful in shooting me down.

It was a great surprise to me when I got wind that my friend Jack Edkins was nearby with a South African Air Force twin-engined Marauder bomber squadron. He and I had been together for a couple of years on my father's farm, until I left to go to Cape Town to commence my training for Christian service at the Bible Institute of South Africa. He had joined the SAAF soon after me, trained as a navigator and then served in the North Africa campaign with No. 12 SAAF Boston Squadron. Now he was a captain and chief navigator with No. 24 SAAF Marauder Squadron. We had not met for a couple of years, so I went over to see him as soon as I could. Many of his

Lt Betton's photo shows the explosion of Franklin's rockets and his plane in the distance (top right) making its get-away from ack-ack fire. The ack-ack gunners got one of our Beaufighters. I should have been killed too, but the 20 mm cannon shell hit the one foot square 5 inch-thick piece of armoured glass right in front of my face – the only armour in my Beaufighter. If it had not been there, my head would have been blown off.

colleagues had been shot down and killed or taken prisoner, but he had survived.

He told me the amazing story of one of their air gunners. One day they noticed anxiety written all over his face. On being questioned, he said he knew he was not going to survive their next raid over enemy territory. Those who spoke to him persuaded him to see his CO and ask to be replaced by someone else. He was very reluctant to do so, but he finally gave in. Another air gunner took his place. But his conscience did not give him any peace. He felt he was sending another man to his death. He went back to see his CO and asked to be reinstated. After a discussion, it was agreed. When the squadron took off, everyone was wondering what would happen.

When, hours later, the time of their return had come, eyes were straining to count the returning aircraft. They were all there. None had been shot down. They landed and returned to their dispersal bays, and the aircrew began to clamber out. But from one of these bombers, a dead man was carried out. It was the air gunner. A stray piece of shellfire had got him!

The Mosquito miracle

Years later I heard a similar story, but with a very different ending. Reg Cousins told me what happened to him when he was a navigator in an RAF Mosquito squadron. They had been attacking a target in Germany close to the Swiss border, when their aircraft was hit with ack-ack fire. They lost all power in one engine and knew they would not make it all the way back to England, so they decided to head for Switzerland, hoping to find somewhere to land at night. There was a full moon to give enough light.

Reg just knew that his hour had come. He had known early that day, when he had got up. He was so certain that this was to be his last day on earth, and that he would not return from their next raid on Germany, that he packed up his belongings and wrote a letter home.

Once they felt certain they were over Swiss territory, they looked hard at the indistinct ground below them for a field on which to land their Mosquito plane safely. Then, suddenly, their remaining engine spluttered and failed. Now an immediate decision had to be made. There was nowhere suitable for a safe landing. Then quite suddenly Reg started to pray. He said if God would get him out of this, then he would give his life to God and serve Him.

As the plane, now with no engines, began to descend rapidly, it became obvious to Reg and the pilot that a crash was inevitable. They hit the ground hard and the wooden construction of the Mosquito broke up, with the engines being torn out. All that was left intact was the cockpit. They both climbed out unhurt!

Psalm 91

When I left South Africa to go to Italy on 'active service', my father gave me a small, compact Bible. On the flyleaf he wrote in red capital letters selected verses from the Psalm 91. I have long since lost that bible, but these are, I believe, some of the words he chose for me:

> *We live in the shadow of the Almighty, sheltered by God.*
> *He is my place of safety.*
> *He is my God and I trust Him.*
> *He protects.*
> *He rescues.*
> *He will shield you.*
> *He orders his angels to protect you where you go.*
> *I will satisfy him with a long life.*

Those words, which were real to me when I first saw them, became even more alive after those two close shaves during my first days with No. 19 Squadron.

I was only hit twice more by enemy fire. On one occasion I had just released my eight rockets and was trying to escape the fire of the ack ack guns, when my right foot was suddenly and violently knocked off the rudder. Wondering what had happened, I waited until we got out of the range of all those guns. I took off my heavy leather glove and the silk glove that we also wore. I then reached down to touch the thick leather sole of my flying boot.

My fingers recoiled instantly as they touched a very hot, small piece of shrapnel that had become imbedded in the sole of that boot. It was hard to believe that such a small piece of shrapnel could hit my boot with such force that it could actually imbed itself into that hard leather. It had been a close shave. It could easily have hit my body, with disastrous results.

One of our other pilots was not so fortunate. He was hit in the shoulder and never flew with us again. Dickie, who had been with us when we sank the SS *Kuckuck*, was shot down and killed very soon afterwards when we attacked the castle at Cernik.

Then there was van Dyke, who was able to bring back his Beau after enemy fire had made a huge hole in the back of his right wing. But Kruger was not so fortunate when we made an attack on a railway siding, where the trucks were being filled with fuel from this fuel depot. He was shot down there, but he and his observer-navigator, cum wireless operator cum air gunner, survived the crash. They were unharmed but, of course, taken prisoner.

CHAPTER 10

Silencing Naval Guns & Destroying a Nazi Headquarters

Silencing naval guns

We repeatedly attacked the concrete, protected installations for the huge guns on Lussino Island. They were situated on the very top of the high north and south hills of Lussino Island, close to the Yugoslav mainland.

Those guns virtually controlled that part of the Adriatic and were a tremendous threat to all shipping. The Navy asked us to put these guns out of action. Our rockets were not powerful enough to do any real damage to these gun installations, because they were so heavily protected by the thick concrete. Our aim was to attempt to be so accurate with our rockets that some of them would find their way into the small openings and explode inside, killing the gunners and damaging, if not destroying, the guns.

In one instance eight Beaufighters of No.16 Squadron and another eight from our squadron

The Allied naval forces were desperate for the Balkan Air Force to silence the Nazi gun emplacements and their huge guns on two hills on Lussino Island that were a major threat to all shipping in this northern part of the Adriatic. Don Tilley led our section of four to the gun emplacement on the southern hill, while another section attacked the northern hill position. Don's and my explosions can be seen and Major Black's Beau is seen as a speck just before he fired his rockets. I wrote at the time: 'Bags of flak, but none of us hit.' And a message came from the Navy: 'Very, very thrilled and pleased with the attack. Beaus did a splendid job.'

We were only able to damage the guns and not destroy them because they were protected by thick concrete roof and walls. The damage we caused was quickly repaired and they began to fire again, so we had to return time and again. Every time we attacked there seemed to be more guns firing at us. No doubt some of the 140 guns at Fiume (now renamed Rijeka) had been brought over to defend those important Nazi naval guns. On this occasion I could not see the guns as the whole of the concrete gun emplacement area had been cleverly covered with camouflaged netting. But I knew from previous attacks exactly where to aim.

attacked the gun positions on both hills at the same time. They came in from the north, and we came in from the south. We did all we could to ensure that our attacks from the open sea surprised our enemy, for example by arriving at different times and from somewhat different directions, or by approaching at sea level. We would also fly towards the island of Lussino as low as possible and then, at the very last minute, pull up with full power to 1, 000 ft (300 m) and dive onto our targets on these high hills. Following this we would get our speed exactly right to 220 knots, all the while searching frantically for those slits in the concrete gun emplacements.

We were always successful in putting the heavy guns out of action for a while, but the Nazis obviously thought the gun positions were so very important that they would work hard to repair all the damage we had caused and get them working again. They also brought in more and more ack-ack guns from mainland Yugoslavia, perhaps from the nearby port of Fiume, where Partisans

As I took this photo I was watching the two Beaus ahead of me making their attack. By the time I came in as No. 3 there was plenty of flak bursting on my port wingtip and some bursting in front of my windscreen. Fortunately not one piece of shrapnel hit my plane. We came in from a different direction this time but did not catch the ack-ack gunners by surprise.

On this occasion I was waiting in my Beaufighter dispersal bay as standby in case one of our No. 19 Squadron aircraft went unserviceable before take-off. None of ours did. But one of No. 16 Squadron fell out and I was called to fly as No. 2 to their CO Lt Col Eric Lewis DSO, DFC. This was the only time I flew with No. 16 Squadron. I only knew we were to attack the guns at Lussino but from what direction or which site or what strategy I knew nothing. All I could do was watch my leader closely and do what he did. As I came in to attack I could see the gun emplacement clearly. It was a very successful attack and we were only shot at by 20 mm.

RAF Flying Officer Younger serving with No. 19 SAAF Beaufighter Squadron took this photo of smoke from rocket explosions with a hand-held K20 camera from his gun turret. It was taken after the attack on large German naval gun emplacements on the Yugoslav coastal island of Lussino in early January 1945.

informed us the Nazis had 140 anti-aircraft guns. It was demoralising for us that we could not finish off those gun sites once and for all. But we returned time and time again in response to pleas from the Navy, who were so desperate for these guns to be kept silent, as they were sinking their ships and other shipping.

The winter of 1944/5 was very cold. It was unusual for there to be snow on that part of the Adriatic coast. It was cold in our little tents, even though we had a make-do form of aviation fuel heating. Many airfields all over the European war zone were closed from time to time because of the icy conditions. Ours was open most of the time. For that reason our rocket-firing operations and our fine photos received quite a bit of publicity in the Allied press. But our rolled-out metal

The Royal Navy had received an intelligence report that alongside the south-western side of Lussino Island, close to mainland Yugoslavia, a small ship was anchored. Between it and the land were submerged midget submarines that the Navy would like us to destroy.

These two photos show how frustrating it was to aim at a carefully selected patch of water without any sight of our targets.

BEAUFIGHTER OVER THE BALKANS

A grounded Beaufighter under wraps during the foul weather of the winter of 1944 when the targets in the mountainous areas of the Balkans were often covered in cloud.

runway was too iced up and slippery for early morning take-offs. Even when the thaw came to melt the ice, it was still very dangerous.

We lost one of our new pilots on his very first take-off before heading for enemy territory. He lost control of his Beaufighter on take-off, and in his desperation he pulled it off the metal runway too early and crashed into the sea. The plane was never salvaged, and the pilot and his navigator were never seen again.

Italian airmen killed by their own bomb

One icy cold morning I was sitting in my plane in the dispersal bay, waiting for the green light to be shone at me from the high, wooden control tower, informing me that I could start up my engines and get ready for take-off. Meanwhile I was watching the Baltimores of the Italian squadron taking off. As I watched, I suddenly saw one of them getting into trouble on that icy runway. It skidded onto the sand and crashed. Immediately one of the bombs it was carrying exploded. To my amazement I saw the body of one of the crew being catapulted into the air. His parachute, which was strapped onto him, suddenly opened while the body was still flying up into the sky. Then, when the momentum of the blast died away, the parachute carrying the body came to rest gently on the sand. But of course this brave comrade-in-arms was dead. Only his torso

When we followed a railway line looking for a train, we would usually select to fire our rockets in pairs. We would try and put out the engine with the first pair with three pairs left for the rest of the train. If the train was heavily defended with ack-ack guns it was foolhardy to follow that strategy.

remained after that terrific explosion.

The Italians suffered heavy losses – more, I think, than the rest of us. We were told that all the pilots were very experienced. We heard them shouting excitedly to each other in the air over their targets. We were all supposed to keep radio silence, but these emotional Italians found it hard to do. Whether or not their forbidden chatter resulted in their heavy losses due to the Nazis hearing them and then finding out where they were I do not know.

One day they dropped their bombs when they were a few thousand feet above their target. Ack-ack guns began firing at them, and one plane was shot down. The others were so incensed that they dived down to strafe at low level the guns that had fired at them – a very dangerous and courageous thing to do when the enemy gunners are fully prepared and focusing their sights on the aircraft diving towards them. I don't know how these Italians got away with flying right into the barrels of those guns, but they did. I can only assume that the enemy gunners panicked and ran for cover.

This photo shows that the leader's rockets missed hitting the railway trucks. I went in too close, and hit the trucks but dirt and snow from the explosion hit the underside of my Beaufighter and froze. A few moments later No.16 Squadron lost two Beaufighters, shot down at a railway siding a few miles from here.

Three direct hits.

My windscreen covered by snow and dirt

On one occasion, I wanted to be so sure that I had hit a small, isolated target in the open countryside with snow on the ground, that I came too close to my target and did not break away sharply enough. It was a railway line that I was trying to destroy. I was hit by ground under the snow exploding up into the air and hitting the lower side of my wings and the body of my plane. Even the windscreen in front of my face was covered with a thin film of earth. I could not see out.

As I pulled the plane up into the sky, I opened a tiny hatch at the side of that one-foot square armoured glass and stuck my gloved hand through this small aperture to try and get my fingers round to the front. As I tried to rub the mud away, I found that it had frozen hard the moment it hit my cold windscreen. I was only able to clear a tiny patch, not much bigger than the palm of my hand. It was just enough to see through and to enable me to find our way back to base, with, of course, the help of my navigator, Joc Mitchell, who would give me the courses to fly.

Nevertheless, what concerned me was whether I would be able to see enough to land safely. When we finally got back to Biferno and had to approach to land on the narrow metal runway, I found that that clear patch was in just the right place. I was able to land without difficulty. My mechanics were amazed at what they saw. It took them a long time to clean the plane. Fortunately no damage had been done to my strong, metal-framed Beaufighter.

We thought our end had come

On another occasion Joc and I thought our end had come. Our target that day was to destroy enemy gun emplacements on an isolated round-topped hill. I found the hill and could see a trench encircling the hill close to the top, but I could not see any guns. In trying to find them, I came in too close, before firing my rockets with their 60 lb warheads. Hoping I would not be hit by the debris of the exploding rockets, I pulled away sharply in a very steep turn, but I was too late. The force of the explosion hit my right wing with such force that our Beaufighter was thrown on its back. Although I kicked my right rudder hard, there was no response. The explosion had interfered with the airflow, and my flying controls were useless.

Fortunately there was a shallow valley to the left of the small hill. Out of control, our plane, in a flat position on its back, descended into this shallow valley. I watched helplessly as the ground appeared to be rushing up to meet us. With my right foot still holding the useless rudder pedal fully to the right, we were about to crash and be killed. Then suddenly, after what felt like an eternity, the adverse effect on the airflow, that had resulted from the explosion, disappeared as quickly as it had come. The normal airflow returned so quickly, that the effect of my foot hard on the right rudder suddenly caused my stricken plane to flick itself over.

This is what I saw as I approached to fire my rockets. I could see a trench all around this hill but could not make out the gun positions.

This enemy-held position was on a hill with a deep valley to the left of it. My Beaufighter was thrown onto its back by my rockets exploding when I once again came in too close. The valley saved our lives. Miraculously my plane flicked back just before we were about to crash.

It happened so fast that, had it not startled me so immediately, I would not have kicked hard with my left rudder quickly enough, making us flick right over onto our back again from the opposite side. We would have crashed. Poor old Joc. It must have been terrible for him. All he could do was to sit there expecting the end. Our navigators had to be brave men to be able to sit in their seats without portraying any fear, hoping and praying that somehow or other we would be delivered time and again from the jaws of death.

Destroying a German Headquarters – The Plan
We were informed that the Partisans wanted us to make an attack on the Nazi-held town of Trbovlje. The first four aircraft were to destroy all the enemy-held buildings along the street on the right-hand side of the church, while the second section of four, which I was to lead, was to completely destroy a large L-shaped building to the right of the small town. The building stood on its own and should come into view immediately after we skimmed the top of the ridge of hills just short of the town itself. We were told to expect quite a lot of anti-aircraft fire, as this was an important German Army HQ.

Early next morning we were taken down to the dispersals and dropped off next to our aircraft. It was to be my thirty-first strike and the date was 19 March, 1945. As we taxied out I wondered what was in store for us.

On our way to attack a very specific target somewhere in the mountainous Balkans.

BEAUFIGHTER OVER THE BALKANS

Airborne, we closed up into fairly loose formation climbing to a few thousand feet to cross the Adriatic. We kept strict radio silence and crossed the Yugoslav coast at Zara, knowing full well that by then the enemy would have picked us up on radar, but they would not – we hoped – have any idea where we were heading. Our target was a long way into Yugoslavia and we kept well away from large towns and avoided all villages known to be German HQs.

Within about fifty miles (80 km) of our target we dropped down to treetop level and from then on the navigating was done by map reading. A heavy responsibility for the leader. The navigator would call out to the pilot what he was to look for: a railway line, a road, rivers, hills and valleys.

By now the three other Beaufighters of the section I was leading had come into close echelon to starboard. To survive enemy gunfire it was essential that we spring a surprise and get in and out of the target area as speedily as possible.

Suddenly, we identified the ridge in front of us. With my heavily gloved hand – for it was midwinter – I pointed to the ridge to alert my number two that this was 'it'. He would do the same to the pilot next to him. We were now ready. Moments later we skimmed the top of the ridge and to my delight and relief the L- shaped building was right in front of us. Had it been even slightly to the right, it would have meant turning and that would have made it difficult for Nos 2, 3 and 4, who would have had to throttle tight back to prevent coming too close to the plane ahead of them.

Onto the target

As I dived into the attack, I had to make sure that the angle was right and that the speed was exactly 220 knots. More important, my aircraft should be approaching the target without my exerting any negative or positive 'G' on the control column. If I did, and fired my salvo of rockets, it would cause them to whip either up or down and miss what were often very small targets.

In the belly of our aircraft we had four 20 mm cannon, and as soon as I was in range I pressed the button on the control column with my thumb and kept it there. Hundreds of rounds converged on the target area with the intention of deflecting the anti-aircraft gunners from their aim. Then, with my eye on the gunsight and with as much accuracy as possible and at exactly the right range, I lifted my thumb from the gun button and with the other thumb pressed the rocket-firing button. With an immediate ignition charge and a swish, the eight rockets left the under-wing rails and sped to their target, hitting it at around 500 miles an hour (800 km/h).

I immediately broke away sharply to port, hoping to miss the rising debris from my explosion, but in doing so I could not see if I had hit my target halfway up the main wall that faced me. I would have to wait until that evening for the photos – if I was not shot down as I broke away. That was always the most dangerous time. I had often seen the big black puffs of 88 mm anti-aircraft shells bursting around us and felt: 'If it were not for God's protection we would not survive.' I was

As we flew in low over a high ridge, I saw the town of Trbovlte and quickly located the L-shaped building we were asked to attack. Would my rockets find their target?

My No. 2, Lt Franklin, took this photo as he followed me into the attack. It shows the five-foot diameter hole made by one of my rockets. He came in too close and the explosion from his rockets damaged his starboard wing. He managed to fly his crippled Beaufighter back to Italy. He was later awarded the DFC.

This is the only one of our many Beaufighter nose-camera photos that revealed a hole made by one of our 60 pound explosive warhead rockets. For some unknown reason this hole was not obscured by the explosion.

strengthened by the assurance that my father, who had been in the thick of fighting as a British Army officer in the First World War and my stepmother, a former missionary to the Zulus in Natal who hailed from the Orkneys, were praying for me and my colleagues three times a day. I also had the promises of God's delivering powers written out in red ink in the bold hand of my father, on the flyleaf of the Bible they gave me just before leaving South Africa.

I emerged from the enemy ack-ack fire without being hit and looked around to see how my Nos 2, 3 and 4 were faring. I could see them behind me, and slowed down to let them catch up. Nos 3 and 4 were soon once again on my starboard side. But where was No. 2? Franklin was known to be a daring pilot. Had he gone in too close and not been able to break away in time? Then, to my relief, I saw him in the distance. Why was he taking so long to catch up with us? We all throttled back even more, but he took a long time to get to us. Then we saw why. It was a wonder that his 'Mighty Beau' was still flying. His right wing had been badly damaged. Not by anti-aircraft fire, but from debris thrown up by his rockets due to flying too close to the target and not breaking away in time.

Fortunately, Franklin brought his damaged aircraft back over the Adriatic to Biferno and made an excellent landing. He survived the tour and was one of us awarded DFCs. Not that he and I deserved the award any more than the others, but perhaps we were involved in some of the more dramatic air strikes which brought our names to the attention of senior officers at BAF HQ at that time.

A satisfying result

That evening, the photographic department called to say that our photos had been printed, so we made our way to the Nissen hut, not only to look at the pictures, but also for a debriefing. I quickly saw the photo of my attack, taken by my nose camera, showing the L-shaped building and I could

On Christmas Day we officers served Christmas dinner to the other ranks.

It was freezing cold in our flimsy tents in that old olive orchard, high up on a hill over-looking our planes down below on the seashore.

see the tiny outline of a Nazi staff car next to the building. I then saw the photo taken by Franklin. It showed clearly that one of my eight rockets had pierced the main wall, just where I wanted it to hit, and that it had blown off the roof from the inside.

We had been told that our 3 inch RPs with their 60 lb warheads were designed to blow 5 ft (1.5 m) diameter holes in walls and would then explode inside, blowing out all floors and the roof. This was the first and last time I saw a photo like that as all the others were obscured by smoke from the explosion. In the past I just had to take the word of the RP boffins. Now I knew what they said was true.

Once again, we had helped the Partisans to recapture a town.

Unusual winter snow covered our PSP runway at Termoli that ran along the seashore. With no machinery, clearing the snow was almost impossible. Fortunately a thaw set in soon afterwards.

CHAPTER 11

Warsaw Airbridge

Fearless South Africans and courageous Poles

On the summer of 1944, when the Red Army had almost reached Warsaw, the Polish people feared that the occupying German forces were about to utterly wipe out the city. They were desperate and felt their only hope of survival lay in an uprising against their enemy.

Lt Gen Tadeusz Komorowski, known as Bor, was the Commander-in-Chief of the Polish *Armnie Krajowa* (AK), or Home Army, in Warsaw in 1944, and he launched the uprising on the evening of 1 August. A few hours later the AK's radio sent out an urgent request for an immediate airlift of arms and ammunition, as well as an appeal to the Russians to launch their attack.

Churchill was determined to render all possible assistance to the gallant AK, with an immediate airlift of sixty tons of arms and ammunition. The distance from Britain was too far, and with the Russian refusal of landing rights, the only alternative was to use the long-range heavy bombers based in Italy. Air Marshal Sir John Slessor, Commander of the RAF in the Mediterranean theatre, was convinced that dropping supplies on Warsaw was not a practical proposition. His fears were confirmed when on the night of 4 August five of the RAF aircraft that went on raids over Poland failed to return.

On the 5th, Air Chief Marshal Portal signalled Slessor that even a small token gesture could have a far-reaching effect on Polish morale, and on Polish–British relations. Two days later Slessor acquiesced... On the previous night, aircraft of the 1586th Polish Special Duties Flight made it to Warsaw and all got back. The crews reported seeing the Poles on the streets below them waving and jumping for joy.

Brigadier Jimmy Durrant, the South African Air Force commander of 205 Group RAF, which included 2 Wing SAAF, was so uneasy about Churchill's decision and of Slessor's agreeing to it, that he went to see him. It so happened that Churchill was there as well and Slessor took Durrant in to see him. Despite being told by Durrant that he did not think an airlift would be a military success, Churchill nevertheless insisted that it must be done, if only to boost the morale of the Warsaw residents and to smooth future relations with the Poles. His words to Durrant and Slessor were short and to the point: 'From a military point of view you are right, but from a political point of view you must carry on.'

Planning commenced immediately; with maximum fuel loads of 2,300 gallons (10,450 litres) and with a return flight time of between ten and eleven hours, there would only be a 10 per cent

A SAAF Liberator on the Adriatic coast of Italy in 1944, seen with the aircrew standing and ground crew sitting. The parachutes painted on the nose represent the supplies dropped over Warsaw in August. The supplies were attached to small parachutes to help break the fall and prevent damage to the equipment. The bombs painted next to them indicated the bombs dropped by this aircraft over many Balkan targets.

reserve instead of the normally acceptable 25 per cent. The direct distance there and back would be 1,750 miles (2,800 km), but with the long days of summer the enemy coastline would have to be crossed in daylight on both the outward and return flights, providing an easy target for anti-aircraft gunners and enemy fighters. To avoid the main interception areas, a zigzag course would have to be followed. That would increase the distance to around 2,000 miles (3,200 km). With only a 10 per cent fuel margin this would make it a very hazardous undertaking. Late in the evening of 13 August, twenty-eight Liberators and Halifaxes of 31 SAAF Squadron and 178 RAF Squadron embarked on their first full-scale effort, with huge canisters crammed full of light machine-guns, ammunition, hand grenades, radio equipment and medical supplies. Five hours later, at midnight, fourteen of the heavy bombers managed to get through all the flak and reached the drop zones. All the canisters were dropped successfully. Three aircraft were shot down and eleven had failed to get through. By the following day the situation had become desperate for the AK. The Red Army had not launched its attack. The AK had been informed that Himler had ordered the total destruction the old city of Warsaw. That night twenty-six aircraft set out for Warsaw. This time they met even stiffer ack-ack defence and after dropping their canisters they were attacked by enemy night-fighters. Eight aircraft were shot down. The Poles of the 1586th Polish Special Duties Flight, who in the early days of August lost very few aircraft, were eventually almost totally wiped out. Despite these heavy losses, attempts were made whenever the atrociously difficult weather conditions would permit. On clear nights it was not hard to find Warsaw, as flames from the burning city could be seen up to 100 miles (160 km) away.

Captain Senn had dropped his Liberator down to 500 ft (150 m) as he approached Warsaw. His aircraft, which had been lit up by the fires of the city, was repeatedly hit by flak. The rudder control and hydraulic system were shot away, the upper gun turret was holed and a fire broke out in the nose.

Captain Senn, as well as his navigator and top gunner, were all wounded, yet he managed to fly this badly crippled Liberator all that long way back to Italy, where they landed without flaps or wheels.

When SAAF Liberator A-ABLE, also of 31 Squadron and piloted by Captain Jack van Eyssen, was down to 1,500 ft (457 m) and still three miles (4.8 km) from Warsaw, it was caught by searchlights and repeatedly hit. Three engines caught fire, and petrol lines burst and caught fire; even with the use of five fire extinguishers, the crew were unable to extinguish the fires in the fuselage. The propellers of the three engines that were on fire were feathered. They were soon down to 600 ft (180 m). All the canisters had to be jettisoned, but the pilot managed to restart an engine and they were able to climb up to 1,000 ft (300 m). But with pieces of metal falling off the starboard wing the captain called to his crew to bale out. Sergeants Leslie Mayes and Herbert

The wreath laid by Her Majesty The Queen on the Liberator Stone Memorial at Skaryszewski Park in March 1996. The plaque reads: 'In this place on the night of 14 August 1944 whilst bringing help to the Warsaw uprising the crew of 178 Bomber Squadron Royal Air Force Liberator EV 961 gave their lives. We salute their memory.' There was only one survivor, Sgt. Henry Lloyd Lyne.

The Queen shakes hands with Alan Bates, the Hon. Sec. of the Warsaw 44 Club and other Warsaw Air Bridge veterans.

The unveiling of the new memorial on 13 August 1997. A bronze plaque shows a Liberator, a cross and two etchings of Warsaw. It also bears these words (translated here into English):

'On the night of 13/14 August 1944 Liberator EW 105 "G" of 31 Bomber Squadron SAAF was shot down over Warsaw during a drop of supplies for the insurgents. In flames the aircraft landed in the region of Okecle aerodrome. Wounded members of the crew were taken prisoner by the Germans.'

BEAUFIGHTER OVER THE BALKANS

Hudson had either been killed by flak or were so seriously wounded that they were unable to make the jump – their bodies were later found by the AK in the burning fuselage. Lt Robert Hamilton's body was found 200 yards (180 m) from the shot down Liberator. His parachute had opened too late to break his fall. The five survivors ended up at a Russian Divisional Headquarters, where after interrogation, they were driven to a village and interned for sixteen days before being flown to Moscow and eventually back to South Africa. Jack van Eyssen, a retired colonel, lived in Johannesburg, and over the years kept in touch with the people of Warsaw and visited the Michalin Memorial and other monuments erected by the Poles in memory of those who gave their lives for them during the period of the Warsaw Airbridge.

It was Bronislaw Kowalski who first erected a shrine in the woods near the village of Michalin, and this marks the spot where Jack van Eyssen crashed in flames around midnight on 14 August 1944. In his garden, Bronislaw erected another shrine in which a light burned day and night in memory of the three airmen who died. Their remains lie in Cracow cemetery with other South African Air Force, Royal Air Force and Polish Air Force aircrew who all perished in their vain attempt to help the Polish AK free Warsaw from the iron fist of the German Nazis.

The Liberator that blew up

On the wall of a school in Ostrow-Klimontow there is a memorial to another 31 Squadron crew. When the pilot, Major Chokkie Odendaal, ordered his crew to put on their parachutes, open the hatches and bale out, after their aircraft had been hit by *Luftwaffe* fighters and set on fire, Lt Jannie Groenewald handed his captain his parachute pack. At that moment the Liberator blew up and he found himself floating through the air with something in his hand. It was his parachute pack. Hastily he zipped it on and pulled the ripcord, just in time to make a safe landing. His face and hands were badly burned. The AK found him and hid him. A surgeon was found who did a skin graft on his face. When the Russians eventually arrived in January 1945 he was able to return to South Africa.

Many familiar faces were missing on that Christmas Day of 1944 when I paid a visit to see them. One face that was missing was that of a tall, athletic young fellow by the name of Eric Impey. I had got to know him in Cape Town before the outbreak of war when I was a twenty-year-old Bible College student: Eric was one of the 150 young men who came to one of our school and varsity youth camps that I was helping to run. He was one of the lads in my tent. Eric died over Warsaw on the night of 16 August. The day he flew to his death he wrote a moving prayer. He was ready to die.

Eric Impey, who wrote 'An Airman's Prayer' on the 16 August 1944, died that night over Warsaw when this South African Air Force Liberator of No. 31 Squadron was shot down and all the crew were killed. The aircraft, Liberator KG987. Q-Queenie, is seen in this photo, taken earlier that summer. The aircrew and ground crew chat before loading up with bombs for a far-off target over the Adriatic, in the area of the Danube.

This Liberator of No. 31 Squadron of the South African Air Force was so badly shot-up at midnight on 14 August, that the captain despaired of keeping it flying and baled out. His second pilot, twenty-year-old Bob Burgess, who had never landed a Liberator, fought at the controls for three hours. Having lost control a number of times, he gave the crew the option to bale out. They all stayed with him. As dawn broke they saw a small airstrip near Kiev, where he was able to make a safe landing. For this feat he was awarded the Distinguished Service Order.

BEAUFIGHTER OVER THE BALKANS

This is what Eric Impey wrote on the day that his Liberator was shot down over Warsaw. There were no survivors.

An Airman's Prayer
My God, this night I have to fly
And ere I leave the ground,
I come with reverence to Thy Throne
Where perfect peace is found.

I thank Thee for the life I've had,
For home and all its love,
I thank Thee for the faith I have
That cometh from above.

Come with me now into the air.
Be with me as I fly,
Guide Thou each move that I shall make
Way up there in the sky.

Be with me at the target, Lord.
When danger's at its height
Be with me as I drop my load
And on the homeward flight.

And should it be my time to die.
Be with me to the end.
Help me to die a Christian's death.
On Thee, God, I depend.

Then as I leave this mortal frame
From human ties set free,
Receive my soul O God of Love,
I humbly come to THEE.

Bob Burgess wins a DSO

An amazing feat of flying by a very inexperienced 31 Squadron SAAF Liberator 2nd pilot took place soon after midnight on 14 August. Liberator K-KING was already in trouble long before reaching Warsaw. The hydraulics of the rear turret had failed. The blazing fires of the city made them a sitting target for the flak gunners as this large plane lumbered through the sky looking for the drop zone. As dozens of searchlights caught the aircraft, the crew of K-KING felt they were flying through a curtain of very accurate and concentrated flak. It was such an unnerving experience that the captain gave orders for the supplies to be jettisoned short of the dropping zone and began climbing away, but not before the enemy gunners succeeded in hitting the outer port engine, which the 2nd pilot, Bob Burgess, immediately feathered.

As the captain took evasive action he seemed to lose complete control, grabbed his parachute and, leaving his pilot's seat, rushed to the bomb-bay doors and threw himself out. Meanwhile Bob Burgess struggled to regain control when it went into a power dive to starboard. The Liberator was down to 1,000 ft (300 m) before Bob Burgess – employing superhuman effort – managed to regain control.

The artificial horizon had toppled during the liberator's wild gyrations. The compass was useless and the navigator, Lt N. Steed, reported that hydraulic fluid was running into the bomb-bay, from a fractured pipeline. Despite all this, and his inexperience, Burgess kept his head. He and Steed knew that they would be unable to climb this crippled aircraft high enough to clear the mountains that separated them from their Italian base, which was five hours' flying time away. They decided to head for Russia. To keep this Liberator flying at all would have stretched the capabilities of the most experienced pilot, but somehow this very new pilot managed to keep his Liberator from crashing. He gave his crew, Sgts Payne, Lewis, Appleyard and Cross, the option of baling out or staying with him and Steed. They all elected to remain on board, hoping that they would still be in the air when the dawn broke, giving them an opportunity to see the ground – and hopefully find somewhere to crash-land on Russian soil.

It took Burgess three hours of tremendous strain to get the aircraft up to just over 7,000 ft (2,100 m). Then inexplicably she suddenly dived to port again, plummeting earthward at around 300 mph (480 km/h). Fighting hard at the controls, Burgess eventually brought his aircraft back under control. But by then she was down to under 3,000 ft (900 m).

Bob Burgess had managed to keep this virtually unflyable aircraft in the air for four hours. Dawn broke at 5.30 a.m. and all the crew were looking everywhere for somewhere to land. Suddenly there was a shout. A small airstrip had been sighted. Bob circled it eight times and decided eventually to attempt a wheels-down landing. To his own surprise and the relief of his crew he made a good safe landing. Local people told them they were at Emilchino, west of Kiev in the Ukraine. They were taken to the British Mission, and when the full story came out, Bob Burgess was awarded the Distinguished Service Order.

A Miracle landing

One of the most miraculous escapes took place close to the centre of Warsaw on the night of 13 August. Bob Klette was in command of yet another SAAF Liberator. Bryan Jones was the navigator and it was their first sortie over Warsaw. Bob wrote afterwards:

> Warsaw was an unforgettable sight. Flames illuminated the buildings and streets of the city. The Vistula River divided the main city to the west from its satellite Praga to the east. Bridges linked the two clearly demarcated cities. We could visualise our heroic Polish allies waiting patiently for the supplies to be dropped, while another mental picture was of trigger-happy

ack-ack gunners preparing to welcome us. The noise was deafening as the flak thumped against the Liberator and as our own guns fired flat-out. Herbert Brown managed to eliminate a searchlight, much to his delight. Henry Upton was wounded. Number two engine was hit and spluttered to a stop. Then Number three was hit, and stopped. Bryan talked me into position and after our load of canisters had been dropped, we were down to 500 feet when I turned for home.

As they flew away from the centre of Warsaw they were soon in complete darkness. There was no sign of an horizon and the artificial horizon and other gyro instruments had been shot away. Suddenly, in the pitch darkness, they felt a severe jarring and scraping under the Liberator's belly. Bob tensed himself for inevitable death. Later he wrote:

> I wondered: had we crashed? Was I dead and in heaven?' Then I took a quick look to the left and couldn't believe my eyes. Our Lib had made a perfect belly landing on a grass surface. 'My God, we are on mother earth,' I yelled.
>
> We jumped out and ran to the nose of the aircraft, where Bryan had been trapped and was hacking his way out with an axe carried in that section of the Lib. Suddenly the beam of a searchlight settled on us and at the same time a machine-gun opened fire. Three *Luftwaffe* types came and took us prisoner. We had landed, it seemed – on Warsaw airport.'

When Eric Winchester, one of the air gunners, got out of the Liberator and started running for cover, he too was caught by the searchlights, and as gunfire raked him he suddenly felt a searing sensation in his bottom. He was saved from serious injury by his parachute harness. He recalls seeing another Liberator flying low over them in the direction of the city. It was on fire. Years later, looking back on that miraculous escape and the hazards of those days in August 1944, Eric Winchester wrote:

> In those three terrible nights, less than 50% of all the aircraft that set off actually succeeded in reaching the Polish capital. Of these, only thirty-four managed to drop their supplies into the city. In one of the highest loss ratios of the war, sixteen were shot down and a further three crashed on landing. Nearly 100 airmen died.

Years later I made contact once again with my Johannesburg friend, Bryan Jones, without whose help this account would not have been written. Concerning that miraculous landing in Warsaw, Bryan wrote:

> Just before we crashed I felt an urge to reach out for the army tin hat which we were obliged to take with us, but never wore. I would not have survived that slightly nose down crash a few seconds later, if I had not been wearing my tin hat. Like you, I too had praying parents and I had their gift of a small Bible, with all its rich promises of protection with me in our

Fifty years after Bryan Jones' Liberator was crippled by ack-ack over Warsaw and miraculously landed itself, this South African giant visited us after being in Warsaw for one of their annual commemoration days.

Liberator G-GEORGE. It survived the POW camp and is still in my possession.

After the crash, whilst lying down on the grass as the Germans closed in to capture us, I prayed: 'Lord, if you get me out of this hell-hole I will dedicate my life to your service.'

Bryan kept his promise. He became one of the ministers of a large church in Johannesburg. In 1994 he and others who flew on the Warsaw Airbridge were in Warsaw to attend the 50th Anniversary and were hosted by the Polish Air Force. They were given – as Bryan put it 'a marvellous, emotional reception'. Prior to that Bryan and a number of other South African Air Force aircrew were honoured during a full-blown medals parade at the SAAF Headquarters at Voortrekkerhoogte, near Pretoria, with the Warsaw Insurrection Cross.

Three of the crew of the 'Liberator that landed itself'. Left to right: Bob Klette, pilot; Bryan Jones, navigator; Eric Winchester, air gunner, and also another Warsaw Air Bridge veteran, navigator, John Colman.

BEAUFIGHTER OVER THE BALKANS

The Warsaw operations bled half a dozen fine squadrons to death, with appalling losses. It has been estimated that 150,000 Polish civilians died in Warsaw. The graves of the Polish, British and South African airmen who in their compassion and selfless devotion to duty gave their lives for the people of Warsaw are still tended and remembered not only by the generation that recalls their deeds, but also by their children. On All Souls' Day and on anniversaries of the Rising, the children cover the graves with flowers and light candles in memory of those who died. In August 1994 members of the Warsaw 44 Club, whose Honorary Secretary, Alan H. Bates DFM, served as an RAF air gunner with 31 SAAF Squadron, were present at the dedication of the crash site plaque of Bob Klette's Liberator K-KING.

POLISH HEROISM OVER WARSAW
(August–September 1944)

Poles fight in Britain

At the outbreak of the Second World War most of the trained flying and ground staff of the Polish Air Force made their way to the Allied lines. By April 1940 over 8,500 Polish airmen had reached France. From there, along with 17,000 escaped soldiers of the Polish Army, they were transported by air and by sea to England.

Polish pilots then played a vital and significant role in the Battle of Britain. They were the largest non-British group in Britain's Fighter Command and they soon made a name for themselves as heroic fighter pilots.

Dispatchers show how they dropped supplies over Warsaw through a specially made hole in their Halifax.
(Air Bridge Assoc.)

Two Polish bomber crews became the Polish C Flight of the RAF 138 Special Duties Squadron until 4 November 1943, when C Flight became independent as the Polish 1586th Special Duties Flight, attached to RAF 334 Special Operations Wing. They were sent shortly afterwards to Tunisia. Their role was to drop arms and ammunition to Partisans. Their Halifaxes and Liberators were modified for air-drops by large holes being cut in the belly of their aircraft to make for easy dropping of supplies over small target areas. The huge bags in the aircraft and the canisters on the bomb racks were attached to parachutes to break the fall and prevent damage to the supplies. Agents were occasionally parachuted behind enemy lines using the same exits.

The gun turrets in the nose of their aircraft were removed and replaced with glass to make observation easier for navigators, who were also responsible for identifying the areas for air-drops.

At Campo Casale

On 22 December 1943, the 1586th Special Duties Flight was moved to Italy, to an airfield close to the Adriatic coast, at Brindisi, called Campo Casale. They were now much closer to their air-drop targets. They could reach all parts of Yugoslavia and into Poland and Austria. 334 Wing became part of the newly formed Balkan Air Force on 7 June 1944, under Air Vice-Marshal Elliot, with headquarters in Bari. The BAF with its ten squadrons was just one part of the multinational Mediterranean Allied Air Forces, headed by USAAF Lt Gen Ira Eaker. His deputy was Air Marshal Sir John Slessor, Commander-in-Chief of the RAF in the Mediterranean and also of the South African Air Force, which came under the operational command of the RAF.

Eugeniuaz Arciuszkiewicz, a major in the Polish Air Force, was given command of the 1586th at this time. When word got through to him on the 1st August that the Poles in Warsaw had risen to fight against the occupying Germans for their freedom and were in urgent need of guns and ammunitions, as well medical and other supplies, he was in a dilemma.

Of his twelve-man crews, seven crews had completed their second and some had completed their third operational tours of duty and were due to return to England for rest. In addition, most of his aircraft were due to be sent to Algiers for major inspections and maintenance. So for a time he could only expect to have eight aircraft and five crews. His dilemma ended next day – the 2nd – when Sosnkowski, his own Commander-in-Chief, ordered that every effort must be made to help the AK in Warsaw. The Warsaw uprising came as a complete surprise to everyone.

Losses will be too high

Slessor agreed with Brigadier Jimmy Durrant, the South African commander of 205 Group, that the losses would be too high, but Slessor was under pressure from every direction. The Polish

President Rackiewicz had appealed to Britain for an airlift of arms and ammunitions for the AK in Warsaw. Churchill, who admired the Poles for their heroism, felt strongly that Britain must not let them down at this crucial time. He had committed the BAF to this task by sending a signal to Marshal Stalin in Moscow, telling him that an initial drop of sixty tons of guns and ammunition to the AK in Warsaw was about to be made. He also made it clear that the AK urgently needed the help of the Red Army, which was so close to Warsaw, but was just biding its time. Stalin was also told that this uprising by the Poles in Warsaw would greatly help the Red Army in its advance against the German enemy.

On the 4th – the very day that Churchill sent his signal to Stalin – five of the aircraft that took off for Poland did not return. This reinforced Slessor's fear that the planned air-drops over Warsaw would not be successful and would result in a great loss of aircraft and crews. But there was nothing he could do. The air-drops over Warsaw had to go ahead.

The Poles in action

When the Polish Special Duties Flight made its immediate response in early August, it was not attacked by enemy night-fighters and the ack-ack was comparatively light. But within a few days all that had changed. The Germans brought in large numbers of ack-ack guns, many searchlights and night-fighters. From then on the enemy defences were so powerful that more and more aircraft were lost – fifty-three in a month. The Poles sustained the greatest loss of nineteen aircraft – six Liberators and thirteen Halifaxes. No. 148 RAF Squadron lost thirteen Halifaxes. No. 178 RAF Squadron lost five Liberators. No. 31 South African Air Force Squadron lost eight Liberators and 34 SAAF lost three Liberators. The Americans who came in later with high-level daylight drops, lost two Flying Fortresses and three Mustang fighters.

Although the cost in human life and aircraft was so high, a large amount of ammunition and guns did reach the Poles. It is estimated that the loads carried by ten aircraft provided basic equipment for a Polish army battalion.

Slessor and Durrant, who predicted great losses, were proved right by 17 August. Seventeen of the ninety-two aircraft sent to Warsaw were lost there. Three others crashed on their way back to base. Most of the others had been hit and many of the aircrew had been wounded. Slessor then ordered all flights to Warsaw to be stopped, but allowed flights to other parts of Poland to continue.

General Sosnkowski

The Polish general would not accept Slessor's order and insisted that the Polish crews of the 1586th Special Duties Flight should carry on. He also said that crews from the 300th Polish Bomber Squadron of the RAF Bomber Command in England must be transferred to Italy to make up the losses incurred by the 1586th Flight.

The weather then became so foul with fierce winds and violent hailstorms that not even the Poles attempted to fly on 19 August. But on the 20th, despite bad weather reports, four of their aircraft took off from Campo Casale for Warsaw. Only three got to their target. A German night-fighter shot down the fourth on the way there. The fires of Warsaw were burning fiercely but despite the fires and pall of smoke they dropped their loads of supplies at rooftop level. One of the three remaining aircraft had two of its engines shot up and it crash-landed on its return flight to base.

Polish Crew Decorated

What must rate as one of the most outstanding flying feats of the Second World War took place just before midnight on 27 August and into the early hours of the 28th. Liberator SKG 927 was piloted by Warrant Officer Jastrzebski, an experienced Polish pilot, who had commenced his flying training in Poland with the Polish Air Force before the outbreak of the Second World War and was among those who made it to Britain. He was on his second operational tour. With him was another experienced pilot, Flt Lt Jan Mioduchowski. The flak was accurate as they were lit up by the burning fires of Warsaw.

The German searchlights also picked them up easily. They had come down so low that they had to pull up to get over some of the higher buildings. The one gunner who doubled as the dispatcher, switched on a light to be able to see more clearly as he prepared himself to drop their load of supplies. Suddenly a searing pain shot through his arm. Bednarski had been hit. The other members of the crew felt it was because he switched on a light, but as the huge plane with its bulk was obviously clearly seen in the light of the fires and by the searchlights, Bednarski would most probably still have been hit even if he had not switched on that light. By the time they had dropped their load S – SUGAR was almost unflyable, it had been hit so many times.

On attempting to increase engine power, the pilots found the throttle controls had all been severed by flak. But fortunately they were already set at almost full power anyway. The outer port engine was also damaged, and when they attempted to feather it, they found that system was not working either. Nor could the belly doors be closed because the hydraulic oil tank had been hit, too. The turret was also out of action. Then further bursts of ack-ack fire hit the Liberator, causing a fire in the starboard inner engine. The wireless had also been hit and it was impossible to contact base. The flaps, too, had been hit and rendered useless.

Despite being so crippled, this Polish crew managed to keep their Liberator in the air on that dark night. With only two engines working and with no throttle controls functioning at all, they did not expect to make it back to base, which was five hours' flying time away. Nor did they think their fuel would last out. It was a long night as they struggled to keep their badly shot-up aircraft airborne. It was a great relief when dawn eventually broke. By this time they began to think they might have just enough fuel to get back to Campo Casale.

When at long last they could just make out their base in the distance, their fuel tanks were reading empty. Now they were wondering if it would be possible to make a safe landing. Would they survive an attempted landing? The pilots made their approach without flaps at 160 mph for fear of stalling. On touching down safely they found they had no brakes, so they immediately cut the ignition switches because they could not reduce engine power. But as the engines had been running for so long at high revs all the way from Warsaw, they were badly overheated and switching off the ignition had no effect.

The pilots knew that unless they could swing the aircraft around, they would run off the end of the runway into the sea and all be drowned. Both pilots applied full right rudder and managed to swing the heavy bomber off the runway on to ground that was so soft that the aircraft slowed down rapidly, despite being on full power on their two remaining engines.

As they swung the Liberator around 180 degrees, first the nose-wheel sheared and then the glass nose broke up. To their amazement a huge stone crashed into the plane. Had the crew not all been directly behind the pilots at this time that rock would have probably killed one or more of them. Then the starboard undercarriage gave way and as the aircraft came to a grinding stop the remaining port engine caught fire. They all quickly scrambled out of the

Liberator 'S' KG 927 of Polish 1586 Special Duties Flight was crippled over Warsaw on 28 August 1944. It was amazingly flown for five more hours back to base at Campo Casale (Brindisi) and successfully crash-landed, despite only flying on two engines whose throttle controls had been shot away. It also had no flaps and no hydraulics.

As this Liberator was swung off the runway, it scooped up a large rock that went through the glass nose and might easily have killed some of the crew.

Had the two pilots not been successful in swinging their Liberator around at full throttle, they would have gone over the cliff into the sea.

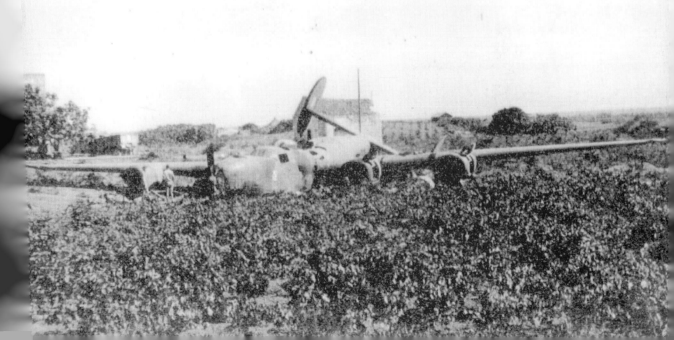

Left to right: N. Nowicki, wireless operator on his second tour; K. Kleybor, navigator, killed shortly afterwards; J. Jastrzebski, pilot, lived in Surrey. R. Ruman, rear gunner; B. Bednarski, dispatcher/rear gunner; wounded over Warsaw; M. Mioduchowjski, pilot; S. Szczerba, engineer. All, apart from Nowicki (who was on his first flight to Warsaw), were awarded DFCs or DFMs, as well as the Polish Virtuti Militari Silver Cross.

wreck, thanking God that they were all alive.

Ruman, one of the rear gunners, who later went to live in Blackpool, and ran the Polish Association up there, told me that he was so grateful that he had escaped death that he kissed the ground as soon as he managed to get out of his irreparably damaged Liberator.

The pilot Jastrzebski, who also remained in England after the war, changed his name as his Polish name was unpronounceable to the British, to the name Morton and went to live in the small Surrey village of Smallfield. He told me that he is convinced that their survival was a miracle. It was always his practice, he told me, to raise his head in thanksgiving to God, on getting safely away from his targets. They were all awarded the Polish decoration for valour – the Virtuti Militari Silver Cross, and six of them were awarded British Distinguished Flying Crosses and Distinguished Flying Medals.

Nowicki, the wireless operator, did not receive a DFM; no doubt, because, unlike all the others who had flown to Warsaw many times, this was his first flight with this crew.

A tribute to the Polish airmen

After the war Air Marshal Slessor wrote *Recollection and Reflections*. This is what he wrote about the Poles:

> The thing that stuck in my memory most was the unusual heroism and sacrifice of the Polish unit. They knew quite well that they could not save the situation, but felt they had to do all they could to help the Home Army. This episode of war shows the heroism of General Bor, his Warsaw army and also Polish, South African and British airmen, who despite heavy

J. Jastrzebski, pilot of Liberator 'S' KG 927 on the night of 27/8 August 1944, receiving the Polish Virtuti Militari Silver Cross.

J. Jastrzebski wearing the Polish Virtuti Militari Silver Cross, the Polish Cross of Valour and three bars and the British Distinguished Flying Cross.

losses in the face of impossible obstacles did what they could, to deliver supplies to fighters for freedom. I feel one of the shameful acts of Russians was their refusal to allow the use of the aerodromes under their control to be landed on by damaged aircraft and to care for the wounded. They refused my pleas, and damaged aircraft with wounded had to try to get back to base 750 miles away, in the dark and over enemy territory rather than at airfields closer to Warsaw.

Jastrzebski and his crew were given a few days' break after their miraculous crash-landing but returned to fly to Warsaw yet again. By this time the people of Warsaw were being starved to death. Churchill later recorded that 15,000 of Warsaw's Home Army of 40,000 perished in their brave uprising. The AK eventually signed their surrender to the Germans on 2 October. In one of the last AK broadcasts before the surrender, London heard the despairing cry from Warsaw:

We were treated worse than Hitler's satellites, worse than Italy, Rumania, Finland. May God who is just, pass judgment on the terrible injustice suffered by the Polish nation, and may He punish accordingly all those who are guilty... Immortal is the nation that can muster such universal heroism. For those who have died have conquered, and those who live will fight on, will conquer and again bear witness that Poland lives when the Poles live.

In addition to the 15,000 Polish Home Army who died, it has been estimated that 150,000 Polish civilians also died in Warsaw.

Winston Churchill knew from the beginning that the airlift was not viable, but was convinced it had to be done for the sake of the valiant Polish people. That their own airmen were so heroic – along with the British and South Africans – gave heart to the Polish nation in their darkest hour.

The memory of all the heroic airmen who gave their lives in their vain attempt to save Warsaw is honoured every year with thanksgiving services in various places around Warsaw where memorials have been erected to remember those who died there.

The unveiling Ceremony of the Memorial to the Warsaw supply drop at Kracinski Place on 1 August 1994. Left to right: Wing Commander Gordon Pryor of 148 Special Duties Squadron RAF;. Tadeuesz Ruman, much decorated rear gunner of Polish Special Flight No. 1568; Alan Bates, bomb aimer in Bob Burgess' crew.

This very young woman with her gun and horse was just one of many Polish women AK soldiers. (Air Bridge Assoc)

CHAPTER 12

Sinking the SS *Kuckuck* & Blitzing Cernik Castle

Sinking the SS *Kuckuck*

The Balkan Air Force HQ based on the Adriatic coast of Italy received an urgent request from the Royal Navy in February 1945. A German ship, the 4,200-ton SS *Kuckuck,* was being fitted with large guns in the Yugoslav port of Fiume. If it was not sunk before it left port it would be hard to track down, and being possibly the fastest ship in the Adriatic at this time it would become a threat to Allied shipping. The Allied naval forces were weak in the Adriatic as their severely stretched resources were fully engaged in other theatres of war. No adequate ship could be spared to deal with the *Kuckuck.*

It was known from reports that had come through from Yugoslav Partisan forces that Fiume was heavily defended. They reported that around 140 anti-aircraft guns were defending that immediate area – 20 mm, 40 mm and 88 mm guns were strategically placed to deal with Allied air attacks.

Senior officers at the Balkan Air Force Headquarters decided that as Fiume was so heavily defended, it would be far too dangerous to send in low-flying, rocket-firing Bristol Beaufighters from either of the two South Africa Squadrons based at Biferno, so they sent in a squadron of high-flying bombers instead – but they failed to damage the *Kuckuck.*

It was then that they called in Don Tilley for consultations. He had recently become the CO of 19 South African Air Force Beaufighter Squadron, which was part of the Balkan Air Force. He was a very experienced Second World War pilot and had distinguished himself at Malta, whilst flying with 39 Squadron, having sunk a large tonnage of enemy shipping. This included at least one oil tanker that General Rommel needed so desperately to replenish his depleted stocks of fuel. Don Tilley had been awarded the Distinguished Flying Cross twice during his time at Malta. His advice was sought over the plans to attack the *Kuckuck,* and he said his squadron would take it on. When asked if it would be like a 'suicide' attack, with so many guns ready and waiting for another attempt to sink the *Kuckuck*, he said he would work out a plan.

Late that afternoon, 23 February 1945, he selected four experienced pilots, including himself, who had proved themselves to be cool headed under attack and capable of hitting small targets. They had to be pilots who could fly in very close formation so that all the aircraft could come

Our control tower where a green light would be flashed at us when we were to leave our dispersal bays to make our way to the end of the runway. There was strict RT silence.

and go so quickly that the ack-ack gunners would be taken by surprise. He chose Major Geater, Captain Dickson and myself.

We met with our navigators in our Nissen hut operations room, where we studied a large map of Yugoslavia. His plan was not to attack from the sea. That would be impossible. We would more than likely all be shot down before we reached the *Kuckuck*. Instead we would attack from the mainland, which hopefully would come as a complete surprise. Providing we held close formation, got through quickly and weaved our way out to sea and out of range of the deadly 88 mm guns, we should all get back safely. Normally eight aircraft would be assigned to deal with such an important target, but Don knew that if there were more than four aircraft involved there would be little chance of the others getting back without being holed or shot down.

That evening, back in the larger Nissen hut served as our officers' mess, there was a strange mixture of unusual quietness by those who were not going to attempt to sink the *Kuckuck* the next day, and the somewhat forced jocularity of those who were.

Sleep did not come easily that night. It was mid-winter. Snow was lying in the olive orchard where our small white tents were sited, overlooking the little Italian village of Termoli. Down below in the moonlight we could make out our Beaufighters in dispersal bays.

Joc Mitchell, my navigator, was soon asleep. As a 'Desert Rat' in the African campaign he had served as a soldier and then remustered into the South African Air Force as aircrew. In the African campaign he had faced danger many times. The possibility of being killed was nothing new to him.

The green light was flashed in my direction, and I followed Don Tilley, to be followed in turn by Major Geater and Captain Dickson. After safely taking off we set course for Yugoslavia and

Off from the Adriatic coast of Italy at Termoli to attempt to sink the SS *Kuckuck* in the Yugoslav port of Fiume where it was being fitted with guns. The Royal Navy was desperate for it to be sunk. Heavy bombers had failed to hit it. This important ship was heavily defended with ack-ack guns. To attack from the sea would have been suicide. Would we survive our ground-level attacks? We knew we would have to fly very close to each other and complete the attack very quickly if we were to catch the ack-ack gunners off guard. I was glad I was not flying at No. 4. Would Captain Dickie Dickson survive? He did, but was shot down and killed a few days later.

crossed the coast at Zara. We knew that the enemy would be tracking us on their radar screens and would be wondering what our target was this time. About ten minutes later we descended in a fairly steep dive down to ground level where radar would not be able to detect us.

We carried on for a few more minutes on this course until we came to a wide valley. Turning about 30° to port we headed up this valley at treetop level for what seemed like an eternity. It was going to be very difficult at such a low level to change course again at the exact spot and head for Fiume harbour. Then suddenly Don began his turn and we all came as close as possible for the run-in. We knew that we would not see the *Kuckuck* until the last moment because it was over the ridge we were approaching. As Don cleared the ridge, he saw that the ship was not immediately in front of us, but slightly to our right.

Unfortunately we were in close echelon starboard so Don had to turn into us and we had to pull back on our throttles to prevent us from crashing into him or overtaking him. Don quickly aligned his aircraft for the attack. The rest of us were struggling to get into the right position and get our speed right, with no negative or positive 'G' on our aircraft, before letting off our salvos of eight 25 lb solid steel warheads, designed not to explode, but to hit ships with such force that they would go right through, providing engines were not in the way. It was essential to hit the ship just below the water line. I saw Don let his rockets go, but having to concentrate hard on last second manoeuvring I could not be sure if Don's rockets had hit the *Kuckuck* below the water line. It was then I realised that a high crane was in my way and I would hit it with my port wing. I had no option but to raise the nose of my plane slightly. That meant that my rockets did not hit exactly where I intended.

As I broke away to port it felt as if every gun was firing at us – 20 mm, then the brown puffs of 40 mm, and following us out to sea the big black puffs of the dreaded 88 mm. With full throttles I was weaving my way out to sea, hoping to be able to dodge all that was being thrown up at us. I was so absorbed with my attempts to make it as hard as possible for the ack-ack gunners to hit us that I completely forgot that we were flying very low. Suddenly it was as if my eyes were made to look at the sea. A couple of seconds later it would have been too late. The sea was dead calm and covered with a thin haze, making it look like glass. Had I hit the sea it would have been assumed that I had been shot down.

Once out of range of the 88s, I looked round and was relieved to see that Dickie had made it too. We began to close up into fairly loose formation, thankful that we had made it, when suddenly to our amazement the sea in front of us seemed to suddenly open up. We could not believe our eyes. We were being shelled by heavy guns and they nearly got us.

When we got back to base we found that the officers at Group HQ did not expect us to fly back all the way at sea level. When they could not pick us up at the expected time on their radar screens they thought we had all been shot down.

Our photographers hurriedly took the films out of the excellent cameras in the noses of our Beaufighters and rushed off with them for developing and printing.

A truck picked up the crews from the four aircraft. As we drove up the hill to our base I told Don that I had switched on my camera ahead of time, not waiting until it was automatically set off when firing cannon or rockets, so I hoped my photos would show that his rockets had hit where he intended. Then I remarked that I nearly hit the crane and did not expect mine to have hit the right spot. To my surprise Don asked, 'What crane?

'What crane?' I responded in amazement, 'You could not have missed it by more than 20 feet yourself. Wait until you see the photos.' We were always amazed at what we saw in our photos. Going into attack at a couple of hundred miles an hour (320 km/h) and concentrating on one thing only – the target to be hit – gives one very little opportunity to notice anything else.

Sure enough the photos we went to the operations room to see that evening showed from my photograph that Don's rockets had struck the ship in exactly the right position.

Next morning, when Group HQ saw the photos and heard from a high-flying Spitfire that the *Kuckuck* had been sunk, they conveyed the good news to the Navy bosses who expressed their thanks and congratulations. A few days later we heard that Don had been awarded the Distinguished Service Order. An immediate award is a comparatively rare event, reserved for something very special.

Our CO of No. 19 SAAF Beaufighter Squadron, Lt Col Don Tilley DFC and bar, fires his eight rockets with solid steel warheads at just below the water line. They should go right through the ship.

Flying as Don's No. 2 with a finger on the button and firing my four 20 mm cannons, my photo shows that Don's rockets hit the SS *Kuckuck* at exactly the right spot. For Don's brilliant strategy and success despite 140 Nazi guns protecting Fiume, he received an immediate award of the Distinguished Service Order.

BEAUFIGHTER OVER THE BALKANS

Blitzing Cernik Castle

In March 1945, the Yugoslav Partisans, heard that the Germans were planning to hold a strategy conference involving twelve generals, and Cernik Castle had been selected as a central venue.

The Partisans then sent a message to the Balkan Air Force HQ, asking for an attack on this castle as soon as they gave the final word. They hoped that such an attack would result in some of those generals being killed. This was a brave step to take, as the Partisans knew only too well that such an attack instigated by them would inevitably bring reprisals. When they killed a German commandant in a daring attack on a German stronghold close to the Austrian border, 250 captured Partisans had been put to death.

One of the difficulties and tragedies of aerial warfare has always been the possibility – and often the probability – that civilians would be among the fatalities. But in using Bristol Beaufighters for the low-level attacks we could be so accurate when firing our salvo of eight rockets that civilians were rarely killed.

A few days later we received a further message from the Partisans to say that German staff cars had been seen to converge on Cernik Castle. Now was the time to launch our attack. After a final briefing of the eight pilots and their navigators – who also acted as wireless operators and air gunners – we were taken down to our airfield and dropped next to our aircraft in their dispersal bays. We were soon airborne, heading out over the Adriatic for Yugoslavia, hoping for clear weather in the interior where, during the long winter months, some of our specific targets had been covered in low cloud or mist.

As we neared our target area we dropped down to treetop level to avoid being detected by radar. We were all very determined to fulfil the objective of the brave Partisans to the best of our flying abilities. On our battle dress uniform we each wore the distinctive Yugoslav Red Star. We wore it for identification purposes. If we were shot down and found by the Partisans, they would immediately know that we were their allies working with them through the Balkan Air Force.

As Cernik Castle and the surrounding area was not expected to be very heavily guarded by anti-aircraft guns, we did not consider it to be a very dangerous target to attack. But we did anticipate that special guns would have been brought in for such a conference of high-ranking German officers, so we closed in not only to surprise them, but also to get through the target so quickly that they would not have time to get their sights onto us.

If we were to expect to find the castle right in front of us when flying so low, it would require excellent navigating by our lead navigator and some very good last-minute map reading by the pilot himself. Our leading Beaufighter was piloted by Lt Col Don Tilley, who was one of the most experienced pilots and the most highly decorated in the Balkan Air Force.

Quite suddenly, there it was, Cernik Castle right in front of us. We were almost clipping the tops

Steve Schonfeldt took this photo of Cernik Castle just before firing his own eight rockets. Other Beaufighters had just come in from a different angle and fired theirs. We came in from as many sides as possible because the walls were so thick. The Partisans later reported to us that we had killed three of the twelve Nazi generals who were there for a conference.

of the trees with our propellers. When we were within half a mile of our prominent target, Don pulled his Beaufighter up almost vertically for a couple of hundred feet (60 m) and we all followed him up. Then just as suddenly he began diving onto the castle. This was the best method of attacking a target with great accuracy. As I aimed my rockets at the roof of the castle I could see the damage inflicted by those attacking ahead of me.

Then someone broke RT silence. 'Dickie's been shot down.' Captain Dickson had survived that 'suicide' attack on the SS *Kuckuck*, when the air had been thick with ack-ack fire. But this time, despite our being successful once again in making it a surprise attack, Dickie had not made it.

Steve Schonveldt had already made a name for himself with the magnificent photograph that he took of my attack on the fortress town of Zuzemberk, a few weeks earlier. At some danger to himself, his navigator and his Beaufighter, he returned to the scene after his completed attack and took low-level photographs of Dickie's crashed plane. We returned to Biferno, on the Italian coast at Termoli, and were taken to our camp overlooking the sea. There we were told by Steve Schonveldt that from what he could see from the photographed remains of the crashed Beaufighter, there would be little hope of Dickie or his RAF navigator, Flying Officer Brace, surviving such a crash.

Captain Dickie Dickson, who survived when sinking the SS *Kuckuck* a few days earlier, was shot down at Cernik Castle and died, but miraculously his RAF observer, Flight Lieutenant Fred Brace, survived with just a black eye. Steve Schonveldt, at the risk of his own life, went back after his attack to get this photo.

The Partisans were high up on this hill in a Jeep (that had been supplied by the Americans) to watch our attack on Cernik Castle. When they saw this crash they rushed down and found Fred Brace before the Nazis got him. This is another risky photo taken by Steve Schonveldt from a different angle.

On the left, Dickie Dickson, killed at Cernik Castle, and on the extreme right, Fred Brace, who survived. The others all survived: RAF observer, Flt Lt Craven; Lt Col Don Tilley; Major Geator and Lt Widdecombe.

That evening we were notified that all the photographs from the cameras in the nose of our planes had been developed and printed and were on display for us to see in the Nissen hut operations room. We made our way there from our officers' mess, and as we looked at the photos of the crash it seemed perfectly obvious that both men must have been killed. From what we then saw of the remains of the Cernik Castle, our attack seemed to have been very successful. The best photograph of all had once again been taken by Steve Schonveldt.

Next day word came to us from the Partisans who had watched our attack from the top of a nearby hill. They had seen Dickie crash and immediately jumped into the Jeep provided by their American allies and raced down to the scene of the crash, hoping they would get there before the Germans. When they arrived, they found Flying Officer Brace standing there with only a black eye.

The only part of the Beaufighter that was still intact was a section of the fuselage!

Captain Dickson was found still strapped into his seat. They lifted his body into the Jeep and got away as quickly as possible.

Within a few days they managed to get Flying Officer Brace back into Allied-held territory in Northern Italy and he was flown back to England. We found it hard to believe that he could have survived such a crash.

135

BEAUFIGHTER OVER THE BALKANS

Then a second message came from the grateful Partisans. Our attack had been successful and three of the twelve generals had been killed. We hoped that these brave Partisans would not suffer further reprisals. As the defeat of the Nazis appeared to be fairly imminent by this time, the Nazis must have had second thoughts. One of the signs that the war in Europe was coming to an end was the retreat of the German Army. One day we flew to a mountain pass in Albania to attack a long convoy of retreating army vehicles. As we knew that we could not make a surprise attack, we let our rockets go from such a height that I wonder if any of us hit this tightly packed convoy, struggling their way up the mountain pass. I was all for making our customary low-level attack, but on reflection that would have been suicide. All their gunners would have been ready and waiting. Don Tilley was a fearless leader. Had it been a strategic target he would not have hesitated to lead us into such an attack, regardless of the consequences. But he knew that this was not a target that warranted him putting us all at risk.

Just before the war in Europe came to an end on Victory in Europe (VE) Day, with an unconditional surrender on 8 May 1945, I was leading a section of four Beaufighters to attack a remote target near the Austrian border with our rockets. But low cloud prevented us from reaching our target, and so, with our eight rockets still on their rails under our two wings, we turned for home. It suddenly struck me that now that the enemy was retreating, there was a shorter way back.

We often flew out over the Adriatic in this type of formation but always moved into echelon when approaching our target so that we could effectively fly to hit our target from a 'follow my leader' formation.

We were flying very low, just in case we were flying over any enemy guns. Suddenly I saw a number of tanks immediately ahead of us. I called on my radio to the others to prepare for attack. With my finger on the rocket-firing button I glued my eyes on our sight, ready to fire. Then at the very last second, I saw men waving at us and holding up their flag. They were New Zealanders, who had made a spectacular advance.

It was touch and go. Had I not been able to call off the attack with only a few seconds to spare, we would have probably killed some of our Allies with cannon and rocket fire and destroyed their tanks. It would also have been an unauthorised attack, and I would probably have been court-martialled. What a way for me to have greeted VE Day! My memories of that event, which took place sixty years ago, often come flooding back into my mind and send a shiver down my spine!

When I look in the mirror now, getting on for ninety years old and then look at this photo taken when I was a Beaufighter pilot, I can hardly recognise myself!

Flt Lt Dennis Bustin DFC, who served with our SAAF Beaufighter Squadron, gave me this photo just before he died. The account he related to me took place just before I joined the unit. He told me that after they had attacked this town word came through that Winston Churchill's son Randolph had been parachuted into Partisan-held Yugoslavia and was in a little house in this town on that day. One of the rockets hit this house but did not explode because it went through a window, through the room and out through another window. A miraculous escape!

CHAPTER 13

VE Day 8 May & VJ Day 9 August 1945

Fifty-five million died in the Second World War

Soon after VE day I was flown to Cairo, where, at the SAAF HQ, I was told that I had been selected to go to England to do a captain's course on Lancasters. A SAAF squadron was being formed to go to the Japanese war zone. To my surprise I found myself excited at the prospect of flying these famous planes. I suppose I had satisfied myself in flying those 'mighty Beaus'. I was now ready for a new challenge.

It was May 1945. The course would begin in August. On returning to South Africa and landing at Zwartkops, I was given leave and went back to my father's farm in the Great Karoo. To my surprise I found that all I wanted to do was to sleep. It took a long time to get back to normal. When I finished my tour of operations in Italy, I felt so well and strong that I had requested that I should be allowed to start a second tour without a break. But this was refused. And in any case that would not have materialised because VE Day came and the war in Europe came to an abrupt end. My experience of being so sleepy showed me that my body had been going through a strain that I was not aware of until it was all over.

Back where the Bushmen once lived

This rest period was a time of thanksgiving that I had survived. My father and stepmother had prayed for me three times a day and had claimed the promises of Psalm 91. I was sure that I had survived my foolhardiness in those early years of my flying, and my rocket-firing experiences over the Balkans, because of their prayers and Psalm 91.

I had time to wander down to the banks of the Great Fish River and to look through the thousands of stone chippings made in a bygone age by the Bushmen who once inhabited this part of South Africa. It seemed that they had to split many, many stones before they succeeded in getting one that was suitable for their spears, which they needed to stalk and hunt the game that roamed all over this part of South Africa. I was told that even elephants had existed in the past in the Great Karoo. The banks of the Great Fish River were also full of layers of shells, which the Bushmen must have brought up from the riverbed to crack open where they were camped.

We would very occasionally see a Bushman who would come to our farm asking for work. But they never stayed long. After a few days they would be on their way again. I wonder why they all left the Karoo. I think it was probably because they could not stand the cold winters in their unclothed state, when all they had for scanty covering were the skins of the animals they killed. Our summers there were sometimes exhaustingly hot, but the winters could be freezing cold. I loathed those cold winters even though I was warmly dressed. How much more must the poorly clad Bushmen have hated them. That's probably why they went that long distance to the Kalahari Desert.

The prospect of returning to England, the land of my birth, in August 1919 filled me with a measure of excitement. I wanted to meet my father's older brother, Fred, who had served in the First World War as an officer in the West Yorkshire regiment, as had my father. In the Second World War my Uncle Fred, as an older man, served on the home front as a major and was awarded an OBE (Order of the British Empire) for his services to his country.

I had not seen much of England during those first ten years of my life. I was born at Salisbury Plain, where my father was serving at the time. Six weeks later his regiment was moved to York, where I spent the first three years of my life. We then lived three years in Germany, where my mother had a disastrous riding accident on one of my father's race horses. This was probably the cause of a brain tumour that resulted in her death when I was fourteen years old.

After Germany we spent nearly a year in Switzerland, when my father was on sick leave, trying to recover from being gassed in Salonica in the First World War. To escape the cold winters, we subsequently stayed six months in Italy during the winter of 1926/7, on the shores of the Mediterranean. Eventually my father rejoined his regiment, which had been moved to Northern Ireland, to be based at the Hollywood barracks, close to Belfast. It was a year or so later, when his regiment was on the move again (this time to India), that he was invalided out and we went to sunny South Africa.

'Dutch' Hugo – the Karoo's famous pilot

Another farmer's son, also from the Karoo, from the little town of Victoria West, not that far from us, became one of the RAF's most outstanding pilots. He was three years older than I was and saw the war coming and decided to go to England to join the RAF. So he was a fully trained pilot when war broke out. It was nothing short of a miracle that he survived the war. He was Piet 'Dutch' Hugo.

On Piet's very first combat with No. 15 Squadron, he shot down a Heinkel 111. A month before the Battle of Britain began, he shot down one of the famous Me 109s. He was glad to see that the pilot had survived and was swimming in the sea. Piet immediately made sure that he was rescued. He soon won his first DFC.

South African 'Dutch' Hugo became the RAF's youngest group captain.

On 5 November 1941, he was awarded his second DFC. By the end of the war he had been awarded the DSO, the DFC and two bars, the French *Croix de Guerre* and the American DFC. At twenty-four he became the RAF's youngest group captain. On the twenty-third anniversary of the Battle of Britain in an article to the press, Group Captain Douglas Bader wrote:

> When I think of that great South African statesman, Field Marshal Jan Smuts, and of those two great South African fighter pilots, Sailor Malan and Piet Hugo, whose names were household names in this country in 1940, I find it inconceivable that South Africa should have been allowed to leave the Commonwealth.

'Sailor' Malan

Adolph Gysbert 'Sailor' Malan was also born in South Africa's Cape Province. His mother was English. His father was a descendent of one of the first Huguenot families to settle in South Africa in 1694. 'Sailor' was born in 1910. He, too, miraculously survived the war and the Battle of Britain in 1940, when 700 of our planes were lost.

Although such losses almost wiped out the RAF, the German losses were disastrous for them. They lost 1,200 aircraft. By July 1941 Sailor's personal tally reached thirty-five enemy aircraft destroyed and five probables. He was awarded a bar to his DSO.

By August he had been involved in 200 combats since the beginning of the war. By the end of the war his decorations included the DSO and bar, the Belgian *Croix de Guerre*, French *Croix de Guerre*, French Legion of Honour and Czech War Cross. He was certainly one of the most skilful fighter pilots and dynamic leaders of the Second World War.

He eventually settled down on a farm near Kimberley, where he grazed 1000 sheep and ran a dairy herd. I probably flew over that area when I was getting my pilot's wings at Kimberley. Unfortunately, he died very young, at only fifty-six, of Parkinson's disease.

Here then is a very brief account of some others of the many South Africans who excelled in the SAAF in the Second World War.

Jack Frost

Early on in the Second World War the name Jack Frost was often on our lips. In the Abyssinian campaign he shot down two Stukas and an Me 109. One day when he was hit by enemy flak he had in that mountainous country nowhere to make a forced landing but on an enemy airfield, where he crash-landed.

Bob Kershaw saw it happen and in the face of enemy gunfire landed next to him. Jack jumped in and sitting on Bob's lap they got away. Bob received the DSO for that brave effective action.

In the North African campaign Jack shot down four Ju 87s in two days. One morning when he

Jack Frost (right), who was so daringly rescued by Bob Kershaw, congratulates him on being award the DSO for his bravery and skill.

was returning from a Stuka operation, he was shot down by our own troops. It is said that what he shouted over the RT was unprintable expressions of anger.

He was lost during what was described as 'a hell of a dog-fight' on 14 June 1942. By time his score of enemy planes shot down was 14.5 confirmed. He had been recommended a bar to his DFC before he was killed, and this came through later. Jack Frost is remembered not just for his successes in the air, but for his outstanding example to those who followed him of great leadership as a squadron commander.

Lawrie Wilmot

Lawrie was a born pilot who went solo in an Avion after only three hours of dual instruction. He was also a born leader of men. He, too, was in the Abyssinian campaign. He shot down his first enemy aircraft when stationed at Port Sudan, flying a Hurricane as CO of No. 3 SAAF Squadron.

Three months later he became C.O. of No.1 SAAF Hurricane squadron based at Azaza. On 31 January 1941 he led eight Hurricanes and three Gladiators to attack Guru airfield, where ten CR42s were found to be awaiting them. In a dog-fight, five of the enemy aircraft were shot down without loss.

Less than a month later, after destroying seven enemy aircraft

Lawrie Wilmot, who was killed after the Second World War in South Africa when his Mosquito broke up in mid air.

Some of the many Mosquitoes that were so effective in the Second World War. These are from No. 60 Squadron SAAF. (SAAF Museum)

parked on the tarmac on the Italian base at Massawa, Lawrie led three Hurricanes to attack Makelle airfield, when he was jumped from behind while flaming one of the parked enemy planes and shot down. When he clambered out of his crashed Hurricane, angry tribesmen, whose chief had been killed in an earlier attack, would have killed him. Fortunately a friendly Italian, soldier intervened and saved his life. He was made a POW by the Italians but was released when the Eritrean campaign came to an end on 31 June 1941.

Lawrie then became involved in the North African campaign, based in the desert at Amiriya. On 2 August he led his twelve Hurricanes and became involved with a dog-fight against twenty Me 109s and Macchi MC 202s which were escorting Ju 87s. His squadron that day shot down five of the Ju 87s.

Lawrie Wilmot completed this his second tour of operations as the sweep leader to 258 Wing, having been awarded the DSO and the DFC. He returned to command 239 Wing RAF as a full colonel. It was much later, in 1947, when I was at Mtubatuba in Zululand spraying the tsetse fly that we heard that Lawrie had been killed while performing an aerobatic manoeuvre in a Mosquito. We were all convinced that the wings had become fractured because Mosquitoes are of wooden construction and not suited to the dry heat of the Transvaal. That was the end of Mosquitoes for South Africa.

Kalfie Martin
Whenever I think of Kalfie, my CO at Pietersburg when I was one of his flying instructors on Airspeed Oxfords, I still feel embarrassed even though more than sixty years have slipped by since I made those glances at his beautiful young wife, not knowing who she was.

At that time all I knew about Kalfie Martin was that he had been a great rugby forward who had played for South Africa. Now, thanks to Peter Bagshawe's *Warriors of the Sky* I realise what a great man he was.

In the North African campaign against the Afrika Korps, when he was commanding No. 3 Wing, he received this message from Air Vice-Marshal Coningham:

> The good work carried out by your squadrons is a reflection of the efficient control and direction at your HQ. Your bombers are hitting the enemy hard and your work is being watched by an appreciative army.

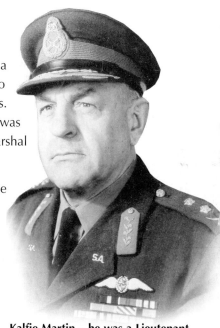

He was awarded the DFC when CO of No. 12 SAAF Squadron and a CBE for his invaluable contribution to the operational techniques and the efficiency of No. 3 Wing. He found some near-fatal defects in some of the bombers and brought into being some design changes.

How I wish he had been with us in Italy. Our Beaufighters had a

Kalfie Martin – he was a Lieutenant Colonel when he was my CO at Pietersburg. It does not surprise me that he went on to become head of the SAAF. (SAAF Museum)

Leonard Cheshire signs the logbook. He learned to fly on Hawker Variants in 1937, as I did too, four years later.

design fault in the tail-plane that nearly cost me my life a number of times. We thought nothing could be done about it. But I am sure Kalfie, had he been with us, would not have been content to leave it at that.

After the war he was awarded the SM, promoted to Lieutenant-general and became chief of the South African Air force. After his retirement he and Col Neil Orpen wrote a series of books about South African Forces in the Second World War. The sixth volume is of particular interest to me. Called *Eagles Victorious*, it is a detailed account of the SAAF war in Italy and the Mediterranean theatre of operations in 1943–5.

While on my father's farm in the Great Karoo, the awesome news of the dropping of the atom bombs over Hiroshima and Nagasaki were flashed around the world. Its total devastation did not fully dawn on me at the

The smoke plume rising almost instantaneously to over 25,000 feet after the atom bomb was dropped at Nagasaki was watched in horror by Cheshire.

time. But it did on one of Britain's most famous Second World War pilots, Leonard Cheshire, who had received so many decorations for valour, including the Victoria Cross. Cheshire, who had been selected to be the British observer on one of those American planes carrying the A-bombs, later wrote:

Before this flight I could not conceive of a man-made flash that would illuminate the cockpit of a plane 15 miles away in the full light of the sun. Neither could I conceive of a ball of fire twenty-five times as large as the Ritz Hotel rocketing up into the atmosphere as fast as the fastest jet fighter in the world and, at the same time, dragging the very dust of the ground up with it.

None of that could I conceive, and yet now I know it is true, because I have seen it happen. I have seen, too, the ball of fire transform itself into a huge luminous cloud that seemed almost possessed of some evil, lifelike quality, as though it were a shapeless monster of the deep convulsed in its agony of death.

When Nagasaki blew up we felt nothing but an overwhelming sense of awe ... something had happened which altered our fundamental concepts of life.

That bomb was a very small one. Its percentage of efficiency was very small. Any future bomb produced will be very much stronger. I think that the figure of 100,000 times as strong is not far off the mark. If there is another war these bombs would destroy every city we have.

Many years later I was seated next to Leonard Cheshire at a dinner in London. He seemed to be very sombre. It has been said that what he saw that day affected him for the rest of his life. From then on he did all he could to save lives, not destroy them.

As soon as I heard of the dropping of the Atom bombs over Japan and the Japanese surrender, I knew that I would no longer be going to England to do a captain's course on Lancasters. When I was recalled from leave and boarded the train for Pretoria, I wondered what was in store for me.

My half-sister, Jean, was at that time in a boarding school in Bloemfontein. It had been arranged for her to meet me at the station to say 'hello' and 'goodbye', when my train stopped there for a few minutes. I had my head out of the window, looking out for her as our steam-drawn train approached the station. I waved as I saw her. On her seeing me, I ran to the door to jump out before the train stopped. Jean was very excited. She had some great news to convey to me. Dad had phoned her that morning, soon after my departure from Cradock, to say that a telegram had arrived for me. It read: 'Congratulations. You have been awarded the Distinguished Flying Cross. The SAAF is proud of you.'

CHAPTER 14

Flying South Africans Home – Cairo to Pretoria

On arrival at Zwartkops I met up with other aircrew from No. 19 Beaufighter Squadron. Franklin was there and he too had been awarded the DFC. He and I were the only ones from our squadron to have received that honour at that time. Some of the others looked dejected and we felt that they deserved this recognition as much as we did.

Years later, when I caught up again with my friend, John Halifax, who served with a RAF squadron on Wellingtons, he told me that when he came to visit me at Biferno, and to go with me on a few days' leave, he asked one of the other Beaufighter pilots how I was doing. His response was: 'He'll either be killed or receive a DFC. He hangs around the target after an attack and is likely to be shot down.'

My posting had been changed from Lancasters to immediately join a DC-3 squadron, to fly those famous planes that we knew as Dakotas. Even then it was an old plane. It had been designed back in 1933. Unbelievably they are still in service today. And so I joined No. 28 Transport Squadron, to be involved with bringing many thousands of South African servicemen back from Cairo. Not having flown Dakotas, I flew on this route a few times with senior captains before being made a Dakota captain myself.

It also meant flying through equatorial Africa, where there were very dangerous storms. Some of our other unsuitable planes had been lost. Any of our forces who did not want to be flown home were given the alternative of returning by ship, but most were in a hurry to return home and opted to return by air. Because so many aircraft were on the move between Pretoria and Cairo at that time, and because we only flew by day, it meant that overnight accommodations had to be found in towns where their landing fields lacked any form of let-down facilities.

Tropical storms were a hazard. We often flew right through them. At first the severity of the lightning was frightening, but we were so sure that aircraft would not be hit that we soon became accustomed to these storms. Tropical storms also tended to burn themselves out within a couple of hours, which made us confident that we would get through them and be in the clear skies once again.

It was not long before I became a Dakota captain, which gave me all the responsibilities for the safety of my plane and my second pilot, wireless operator and passengers. We usually flew up to Cairo almost empty, but on the way back every one of the twenty-eight seats was taken. Among our passengers were those who had spent years in prisoner-of-war camps. They had suffered much, but their spirits were now raised at the thought of soon being reunited with their families. But I am sure those many hours of flying over a period of around five days must have dragged.

Tabora in Tanganyika

One of the places where we sometimes spent a night was a remote place in Tanganyika, as Tanzania was then called, by the name of Tabora. Italian prisoners had been kept there for years. They had most probably been captured early on in the Second World War during the Abyssinian campaign, in that mountainous country that had been ruled by the Italians and we now know as Ethiopia.

They made beautiful wooden trays in sets of three sizes. I bought sets to give as wedding presents and a set for myself, which we used for many, many years. One day after landing there, I hurried to the local market, a mile or so away from our little hotel, to see if I could find any interesting wood-carvings, tom-toms or anything else that might catch my eye. I was hurrying because the sun would soon be setting and in that part of Africa there was almost no twilight.

I was walking fast down a narrow African path, with grass about three ft (1 m) high on both sides. Suddenly on my left, to my amazement, I saw the head of a hooded cobra appear. I could not believe my eyes. Cobras are not usually much more than six ft (2 m) long. Never had I seen a cobra with such a large head, nor one that could, with its large head, raise it so high! I was so frightened by this huge snake that I ran for safety.

In the days that followed, whenever I heard of anyone who had been to Tabora, I asked if they knew anything about that snake. Eventually my enquiries brought a response. One man, who was stationed for a while at Tabora, said that they were driving down a track that was about ten ft (3 m) wide when they suddenly noticed a snake crossing the track immediately in front of them. But they could not see its head nor the end of its tail. They knew it was not a python.

They got out of their vehicle and saw a large hole in the side of a huge anthill. Believing that to be where this snake had gone, they got someone to blow it up with dynamite. But they found no trace of that snake. However, it was never seen again.

Kisumu in Kenya

Another place where we sometimes spent the night was Kisumu in Kenya. It is situated on the eastern shore of a huge lake, the size of Wales, patriotically called Lake Victoria. We stayed in a small hotel built mainly of wood. Constructed on stilts on the edge of the shoreline, the lounge and dining room had large windows overlooking this vast expanse of water.

It was a pleasant place to relax in after a long day of flying. When I roamed through this small market town. I was amazed at how many one-legged men I saw hobbling around. On enquiry I found that they were fishermen who had been attacked by man-eating crocodiles. Many had been killed and eaten. These were the lucky survivors.

Sudan's Malakal – a 'frying pan'

One of the places I hated landing at for refuelling was Malakal on the edge of the White Nile, which had its source at the northern end of Lake Victoria. It gained momentum as its waters rushed down into the lowlands of the Sudan, where it then sluggishly made its way for a couple of thousand miles (3,200 km) to Egypt. Although Malakal was so far from the sea, it was only 1,750 ft (530 m) above sea level and very hot – so hot that our Dakota was like a furnace when we climbed back into it. Our clothes were wringing wet by the time we had taxied out for take-off.

Watching us were the blackest Africans I had ever seen. These men were completely naked and carrying long spears. They always seemed to be standing there on one foot looking at us intensely, the sole of the other foot resting on the other leg just above the knee. It looked uncomfortable, but when I tried it in my shorts and without shoes I found it to be quite a comfortable stance. I remember thinking of Malakal as the end of the world. It was always a place to get away from and up again into the cool upper air.

On one occasion returning to South Africa from Cairo with a full load of servicemen, we experienced some ghastly turbulence over the South Sudan as we were approaching the equator. Virtually all my passengers became airsick and I was beginning to feel that way myself – something I had never experienced before in all my years of flying. In an attempt to get out of it, I climbed higher and higher, eventually reaching around 17,000 ft (5,200 m). But it made no difference. I did not dare go any higher without oxygen. Not finding any relief to our being bounced about in clear air, I dropped down a few thousand feet and rode it out. It was a great relief when we finally landed at that day's final destination.

The heat of the Sudan was so intense, that at its main airport of Khartoum some planes would not attempt to take off in the middle of the hot season in the midday sun. We preferred night-stopping in the very north of the Sudan, a country of nearly a million square miles (nearly 260 million hectares) and the largest country in Africa.

Wadi Halfa on the banks of the Nile was cooler than Khartoum. It was desert country – nothing but sand. The waters of the Nile meandered through this sleepy little town. Whereas the waters of the White Nile were crystal clear at Malakal, the waters of the Nile at Wadi Halfa were dark and muddy, the reason being that the White Nile was joined at Khartoum by the waters of the Blue Nile from Ethiopia to become the Nile proper. The Blue Nile carried with it the rich topsoil from the Ethiopian mountains all the way to Egypt. This caused the fertile soil to come to rest on desert sands, turning it into a 'desert that blossoms as a rose'.

My days in Cairo

On reaching Cairo after that long haul from Pretoria, we were always given a few days' rest in a hotel in the middle of that bustling city. I found it was possible to take a tram all the way to the pyramids. I also found that one did not have at that time to be taken over the pyramids by one of the unofficial guides who were there ready and waiting. Once having found such a cheap way of getting to the pyramids, I took a number of other pilots on subsequent trips to Cairo, out to this remote area.

By then I had learnt to take candles and matches with us. When I brought my first party of other pilots with me and declined the services of the guides, they nevertheless followed us on our walk from the tram to the pyramids, assuming that we would have no option but to use them once we arrived at the entrance and found ourselves in utter darkness. They murmured their disapproval when we got out our candles and matches. We knew very little about these amazing structures at that time. But now, of course, with so much written and filmed about Egypt, a great deal is known about them, even though how such huge stones were cut and lifted into place is still something of a mystery.

If I happened to be in Cairo on a certain day of the week, I would make my way at sunset to a high block of flats in the middle of Cairo, to the flat of a Swiss Christian couple, who opened their home once a week to servicemen for a meal, fellowship and a bit of Bible study. I looked forward to those evenings.

Mr Zinniker was always dressed in white and immaculate. Years later, when the days of tranquillity in Cairo gave way to unrest, I heard that this fine, godly man had been murdered. The whole matter seemed to have been brushed under the carpet by the authorities, and of course the culprit was never found. It was there in the Zinnikers' flat that I met a British Army captain by the name of Rod Frampton. We became friends and kept in touch right up to the time of his death a few years ago.

The Ngorogoro crater

Eventually, when the large numbers of South African servicemen waiting to be flown back to South Africa began to dry up, we began to fly equipment back to South Africa. On one of my trips back I had a Jeep on board. Our route through Kenya and Tanzania took us within easy reach of the famous Ngorogoro volcanic crater. Having no passengers, we decided to fly into it and have a look at all the game that lived there. It was a very fertile crater with lush vegetation. When we came close to the rim of the crater, we were amazed to see that the crater itself was so huge. We would have no difficulty in making a low-level, circular flight in it. We crossed the rim with only a few feet to spare, and, throttling back, we descended at low speed down to the floor of the crater.

Immediately in front of us was a lake. It was white with hundreds of flamingos. Suddenly they saw and heard us coming and spread their wings to fly away. What had been a mass of white became tinged with a beautiful pink emanating from their outstretched wings – a sight to remember!

Just beyond the lake was a small forest of high trees where giraffes were feeding on succulent leaves. Now at low level and at reduced speed, with the noise of our two engines being kept as low as possible so as not to alarm these wild animals too much, we made a gentle turn inside this amazingly lush crater. We saw many zebras, wildebeests, gazelles, hyenas and lions. They would all look up when their sharp ears detected us coming and then run out of our path. Not the lions, however, that were lying in the hot sun relaxing! No doubt they had made a recent kill and at this time were no threat to their prey that were grazing very close to where the lions were lying. When they saw us coming they stood up and watched us but held their ground. They were not going to be intimidated by this large bird that had had the audacity to come and disturb their rest!

As we circled this crater with its high walls all around us, we noticed how steep they were. We could see no path made by the animals for them to come and go as they pleased. Maybe many of them had been born there and would die there, without having had the inclination or the need through drought ever to leave this wonderful place with its protective walls all around them. Those few minutes in the Ngorogoro crater is something I will never forget.

CHAPTER 15

War on Disease: Air Spraying in Zululand

*S*oon afterwards I was greatly surprised and delighted to be informed that I had been selected to become a spray pilot and that I was being posted to a remote place called Mtubatuba in Zululand. After the long train journey to Durban and then the overnight train ride to Mtubatuba, I was met at the station, that was little more than a siding, and taken some miles on rough roads, that were little more than tracks, to the SAAF camp with its wooden huts dotted here and there among the huge gum trees. I was to fly twin-engined Avro Ansons. They were old and had seen better days. Inside there was a huge tank filled with DDT.

Every morning, as dawn broke, when the air was at its calmest, six aircraft would take off and fly to one of the three game reserves. Then, in close echelon formation and down to tree top level, we would 'turn on the tap'. The DDT would come out as a spray covering the top side of the leaves and foliage and then bounce back up covering the underside of the leaves and then hover just above tree top level, before very gradually sinking onto the ground.

Captain Shen, an ex-Army officer with the Agricultural Department, which was monitoring our

When we turned on the DDT tank tap in the cockpit it would come out of this pipe. (SADF PR)

We would spray our DDT at the crack of dawn from about ten feet above the tree tops. As we had huge areas to cover, we would usually use six Ansons flying in echelon formation but well behind each other to judge if the DDT was spreading. We needed windless conditions to be really effective. In the background where we had just sprayed, the DDT was settling uniformly as a mist. (SADF PR)

work, had tsetse fly traps all over these three game reserves. He found that immediately after we had flown up and down a huge area, covering it with our DDT spray, no tsetse fly were caught in his traps, but within a week or so more and more of them would be found in these traps.

A helicopter is needed

It was found that we were very successful in exterminating the tsetse fly wherever we could lay our mist of DDT spray, but we could do nothing in all the hilly areas with our Ansons. We decided that helicopters would be needed to deal with that problem. As far as I can recall there were no helicopters in South Africa at that time. Eventually it was decided to import from the USA two Sikorski 51 helicopters. Two of us, who were experienced flying instructors, were chosen to go to America to learn to fly helicopters and then to teach our fellow SAAF pilots to fly them.

Meanwhile we persevered with our inadequate Ansons. It was dangerous flying. Vultures were a real hazard. They would be perched on trees watching us coming and then suddenly, at the last moment, become very fearful and frantically rise into the air to escape. Had one of these heavy birds hit one of our engines, when we had a full load of DDT on board and full tanks of fuel, we would have crashed into the trees with fatal consequences, as there was no chance of being able to keep a heavily loaded Anson in the air on one engine. But as these vultures began to become used to us, they also learned when they saw us coming to drop from their perch to the ground, until we had come and gone.

On one occasion I experienced another hazard. I was flying into the rising sun at tree top level, with one of my hands shielding my eyes from the glare, when at the last minute, after it was too late to do anything about it, I saw a solitary dead branch sticking out, high above the green canopy of the other tree tops. I crashed into it, and the glass of the landing light on my wing was shattered. It just missed my port engine.

Snakes abound

In this wild part of Zululand there were also hazards on the ground. There were plenty of deadly snakes in Zululand, and they often appeared in our camp. We kept sticks around with which to kill them. One day a Zulu arrived, offering to sell us the skin of a python he had killed. He brought it in a huge roll. We were amazed at its size when unwound. One day an officer from SAAF HQ in Pretoria came for a visit. It was decided to play a snake joke on him.

A large cobra had been killed that day. It was placed under the very large table in the hut that served as our officers' mess, and a heavy stick was conveniently placed nearby. Then when we all sat down with our guest for a meal, it was not long before this prankster noisily got to his feet, ran to grab the stick and took a swipe at this dead snake and then dragged it out by the tail and hurled it out through the door. He replaced the stick and sat down as though nothing had happened. Meanwhile all our other officers, who were in the know, acted as though nothing unusual had taken place! Our visitor tried to keep a calm face, but he had obviously been shaken, especially by the nonchalant way in which the rest of us had reacted. We wondered if that story did the rounds back in his officers' mess in Pretoria!

Most South Africans never play pranks with snakes. Years before, when we had been in South Africa only a short time, we were staying as paying guests on a farm in the Grahamstown area, while my Dad was trying to decide where to settle. One day, while I was in the fruit orchard with my air gun, trying to shoot the birds that were enjoying the huge luscious figs, I came across an almost perfect skin that had just been shed by a large cobra – something they do regularly as they grow in size and they become too cramped in that old skin. I carried it back to the homestead to show my father.

He had always been a bit of a prankster. He had an idea. We would stuff it with cotton wool or whatever was suitable, then intertwine it among the heavy foliage and grape vines that were growing high up on the edge of the verandah. This was done when no one was around. Then, at an appropriate time, when the farmer came home, we called to him excitedly that there was a snake among the vine branches on the stoep (as verandahs are called in South Africa). He grabbed his shotgun and let fly, blowing it to bits. We roared with laughter. He was not amused! He told us firmly that South Africans do not play games like that. Deadly snakes are not to be trifled with.

The petrified Alsatian

One day, after our early flying duties were over, three of us decided to explore an area of jungle that we had seen from the air. It was on the other side of a large lake. We took with us three of our heavy sticks and a large Alsatian. When we emerged from the forest and saw the lake in front of us, we were disappointed to find that we were so close to the middle of the lake that it would take us ages to walk round it. As we were fairly sure it was very shallow, we decided to attempt to wade through it. We thought it was probably too shallow for crocodiles. In our inexperience of crocodiles, we thought, as our eyes scoured the lake, that we would see them if there were any. We also wrongly assumed that they would not attack humans, and in any case we had our sticks! As we began to wade into the lake, our Alsatian began to whimper and refused to follow us. Nothing we could do would persuade the dog to come with us. Eventually I decided to try and carry this large dog. He was put on my back with his front paws on my shoulder. This seemed to satisfy our Alsatian, and I was able to struggle my way through the mud of the shallow lake.

When we got to the other side, the jungle was too dense for us to penetrate without a great deal of difficulty. Then suddenly we noticed a very narrow track. It had probably been made by local Zulus and was now used by wild animals coming to the lake to drink. I happened to be in the lead, when suddenly I noticed that a large python was crossing the path. The thick grass prevented me from seeing its head or tail. Seeing the direction it was heading, I hit down with my stick with all my strength on the grass where I thought its head might be. My stick seemed to bounce back at me as if I had hit rubber. Then immediately its huge head rose up and I had to duck back to prevent it from hitting my face.

The scent of a leopard

Soon afterwards, as we continued on our way, our Alsatian began to whimper again, but this time kept following us. We assumed that this dog could smell a scent that we could not detect. We had not gone much further before we too could smell something. It soon became obvious that a leopard was nearby. The scent became so strong that it reminded us of being close to the lions' cage in a zoo. With our sticks at the ready we, in our foolishness, began to look for it. We never did find it – which is just as well. We realised then that our Alsatian had probably detected the smell of crocodiles in that lake. It was not until much later that I found out that crocodiles had the ability to lie dead still in the water with only their eyes protruding. We decided that we dare not retrace our steps. We would never wade through that lake again. We eventually came out into the open and had to move fast to beat the setting sun. When we eventually got back before darkness fell, we thought we must have trekked eight miles (13 km). Carrying that heavy dog through that muddy lake damaged my right knee, and the more I walked on it that day, the worse it got. The pain still comes back today if I walk too far and is a constant reminder of that day in Zululand all those years ago.

Chased by a rhino

One day, on my one and only visit to the game reserves, three of us were taken by Captain Shen's nineteen-year-old son to see Matilda, a rhinoceros, who lived alone on a small isolated hill. As we approached the hill, this lad asked us to follow him as quietly as possible. He was going to

Kay and I were married in Durban in August 1947. She was one of the van Rij girls that I had known since 1940 when I joined the SAAF. Previously, Kay had married Jimmie Mowat who had been invalided out of the King's African Rifles and went with him and his missionary parents up the Zambezi River for five days in a huge dug-out canoe with five paddlers to a remote Zambian mission station. Kay nearly died there of Malaria. A year later Jimmie died. Kay, a pioneer, was the ideal wife for me with my plans of becoming a jungle missionary pilot.

stalk this female rhino. He got very close without being detected. We were close on his heels, looking at this fine creature. Then our guide picked up a stick, took careful aim and threw it, hitting Matilda on her horn. Snorting, this great rhino charged. We did not know until that day how fast a rhino can move. We flew and scrambled up the first tree we could find. But not this lad. All he did was to duck behind a shrub and keep absolutely still. He informed us, when the danger had passed, that rhinos have very poor eyesight so it is quite easy to hide from them if they charge. Had he told us beforehand, I doubt if we would have had the nerve to do as he did. We would probably still have made a run for it!

We had a fine tennis court and a squash court at our camp among those gum trees. A new pilot arrived, who had never played squash before, and although I could at first beat him at squash, I was certainly no match for him at tennis. He had been the junior champion of the Western

BEAUFIGHTER OVER THE BALKANS

Province of the Cape. He hit so hard that I developed a tennis elbow and had to go to Durban for medical treatment. I was seconded to a Sunderland squadron during my sick leave. When I began to recover, I was assigned the flying job of doing the weather flights every morning at dawn, using the little grass Durban airfield that was conveniently close to Concord, where Kay and I were staying. I had done the 'Met Flights' in Harvards before in Pietersburg in the Northern Transvaal, so this was nothing new to me. Harvards are notoriously noisy on take-off. As I did not want to awaken all those thousands of people living in that area, I found that by taking off at reduced power and getting the pitch just right, I could take off without disturbing anyone.

Sometimes I climbed up on my blind-flying instruments through a thousand or more feet of dense cloud. It was always exciting to break out into a clear sky, with the brilliant rising sun glinting spectacularly on the top of that flat layer of cloud. When I had taken all my readings and was about ready to

Kay and Jimmie's daughter Merle was the flower girl at our wedding, she was only six months old when her father died. I am greatly indebted to Merle, who is a very experienced editor, and with Dr Christina Lawrence edited this book.

enter the cloud once more to make my descent, I would sometimes play around on those slightly undulating cloud tops, pretending they were ground. I would do very low flying above them, making sure that the belly of my havard did not brush that layer of cloud. It was the rising sun that had the effect of making the cloud tops look so solid.

When my mind returns to many of my happy flying days like this, I'm reminded of the words of John Gillespie Magee jnr's poem, *High Flight* , that he wrote in 1941 during those dreadful days of war. Yes, some of my flying was extremely dangerous and could often have been fatal, but the happy memories are there too and with it all, as Magee so clearly indicates, a sense of the presence of God.

More than 600 Harvards were delivered to South Africa. A less sturdy aircraft might well have broken up when I foolishly dived down through that long tunnel of heavy cloud. (SAAF MUSEUM)

Foolhardy flying

One day, when I had climbed through a very, very thick layer of cloud and was ready to descend, I noticed to my surprise a vertical tunnel in the cloud and could just make out, rather indistinctly, a patch of ground. Very stupidly, without a second's thought I flicked my Harvard on its back and put it into a vertical dive, with my throttle right back to keep my speed as low as possible. As I flew down through this tunnel, I suddenly remembered that this was a very, very thick layer of cloud. The speed rose to dangerous levels, but I did not dare slow it down by flying into the cloud, because my main blind-flying instruments would no longer be functioning. They were not designed to operate under such extreme conditions. So I had no option but to keep going down vertically, hoping and praying that my foolishness would not result in my plane breaking up in mid-air.

Fortunately the wonderful Harvard took the strain, and suddenly, after what felt like an eternity, I reached the base of the cloud and was able to ease the over-speeding plane slowly out of its vertical dive. I had to do it very slowly because of the excessive speed. Had the cloud base been low, there would not have been enough clear air space to bring my plane back to straight and level flight. I think I must have been sweating even in the cool morning air, when I touched down and taxied in. On that day I probably appreciated the firm feel of the ground beneath my feet as I walked away, more than ever before.

'Mr Marshall, your flying is too dangerous!'

To my surprise I found that my old friend, Gordon Marshall, who first came to our farm in the Karoo when I was seventeen and he was only ten, was now based in Durban, flying as a pilot with a South African Air Force Squadron on Sunderlands. He invited me for a flight. We took off one day in this, what I thought then, to be a massive boat plane, from the large bay of Durban's harbour. That one flight was enough to tell me that I did not want to fly such a cumbersome plane. Later on, when I again happened to be in Durban, Gordon Marshall told me that he had been assigned to do some low flying amongst the ships in Durban Bay for naval target practice. I did not know what was going to be in store for me that day when I climbed into the single-engined Harvard. Gordon flew just above the water, making very steep turns around those naval ships. It was, I thought, the most dangerous flying exercise that I had ever been on. There was no room for error.

When Gordon rolled the plane from one steep turn to the other side, his vision was blanked out by the underside of the plane. Gordon's flying skill was amazingly accurate. But with an engine in front of him, wings and the belly of the plane below him, all impairing his visibility, I felt it was only going to be a matter of time before we hit one of those ships. I would have liked to speak up, but he was flying as the pilot and I was only a passenger, so I kept silent. Then suddenly the radio crackled and a voice called to Gordon that the Commodore had sent a message, saying the flying was too dangerous. That was the sweetest message I had ever heard. When we landed, I was so airsick that I barely managed to get out of that Harvard before I vomited, something I had never done before. Soon afterwards Gordon became twenty-one and Kay arranged a surprise party for him. I did not reveal to her how close to death Gordon and I were on that never-to-be-forgotten day.

Sikorski helicopters arrive

When our two Sikorski 51 helicopters arrived by ship to Durban from America in their massive wooden crates, I happened to be there and saw them being assembled. When they began to take shape, Kay and I climbed into them one day and took our seats. The visibility all around – or almost all around – was amazing. I longed to fly them. By this time Captain Shuttleworth and I, as flying instructors, who had been selected to go to America to learn to fly them and how to instruct others to fly them, should have completed our training. But at the last moment the SAAF Headquarters staff in Pretoria gave this plum experience to two senior officers at HQ instead. We were annoyed about this, especially when we heard that one of them was supposed to have said that he was only going to train our spray pilots to fly helicopters, but not to be a helicopter spray pilot himself!

My destiny, however, was for something much better and much more rewarding, although at that time I could not think of anything more fulfilling than being a helicopter pilot, training others

My widowed bride with her daughter Merle taking a look at one of the SAAF's two Sikorski 51s. They had been shipped from USA to Durban in crates. I was to have gone to America as a fixed-wing flying instructor to learn to fly them and then to teach other SAAF pilots to fly them. However, I was selected to captain a Dakota on the Berlin Airlift instead.

Testing one of the two sikorski 51s after assembly at the small airfield close to the centre of Durban. (SAAF Museum)

to fly and flying low over the hills of the game reserves, spraying DDT where our Ansons could not go. To my great surprise my CO called me to his office one day to tell me that I had been selected to be one of the pilots on the Berlin Airlift, because I was a DC-3 Dakota captain.

By this time we were accustomed to the dangerous work of spraying DDT at just a few feet above the bush and trees in these old and rather unsuitable Avro Ansons which would almost inevitably crash if we lost an engine.

All the time I was a SAAF spray pilot we did not lose a single Anson. It certainly came close to it when a protruding dead branch that I did not see as I was flying straight into the rising sun, hit and smashed my port landing light just a couple of feet from the propellor.

One of our early helicopters crashed. If I hadn't been flying on the Berlin Airlift, I might have been flying it. (SAAF Museum)

BEAUFIGHTER OVER THE BALKANS

What never crossed my mind was how dangerous it would be to use helicopters to spray at tree-top levels in hill country. From the little I've heard, the Sikorski 51s were successful in eradicating the Tsetse Fly in the hills of the Zululand Game Reserve that was impossible for us in fixed wing Ansons. But eventually after most if not all the Tsetse Fly in the hills had been exterminated, one of the Sikorski 51s came to grief, but the pilot, Lt Wheeldon survived. Some months later the second one also crashed and again the pilot, E.W. Fortuin, survived. 'I wounder what my fate might have been. I might have been flying one of them and not survived. Or a pilot I might have trained might have died. If that had happened I would probably wonder if I had taught him well enough. Maybe it was providential that I left for the Berlin airlift instead.

I was to be away for six months. If the Berlin Airlift continued after that, others would be found to take our places. Although I looked forward to this, Kay and I were not looking forward to our parting. With two children to care for, and one just a small baby, she could no longer fulfil her role of helping to run Concord Missionary Home in Durban. So she moved to Johannesburg, where members of her family took her in. It was not easy for them or for Kay.

CHAPTER 16

The Cold War: Berlin Airlift Miracle

On arrival at Zwarkops I met up with pilots, navigators and wireless operators who had been called by SAAF Headquarters from air stations all over South Africa. Most of us had flown Dakotas at one time or another with either 28 or 44 SAAF Transport Squadrons.

When we were informed that our overseas posting was to be involved with the 'Berlin Airlift' we had no idea that we could be on the brink of the Third World War. Nor did we realise that we were going to be privileged to be part of the greatest airlift in history. We warned our wives that we would be away for six months or more. It was a long haul to Europe in slow Dakotas. We followed the East African route that most of us knew like the backs of our hands. By 25 January 1946 we had flown over 100,000 returning troops on this route. We headed for Bassingbourne in Cambridgeshire, near Royston, where we spent time getting our hands in again on Dakotas before leaving for the RAF base of Lübeck, near Hamburg.

Lübeck to Berlin

Soon after full briefings about procedures, my navigator, wireless operator and I climbed into our Dakota, loaded with three and a half tons of coal in 100 lb sacks to fly from Lübeck to Berlin for the first time. We were nervous about reaching the Fronhau Beacon on the outskirts of Berlin within sixty seconds of our appointed time of arrival there. We climbed up to 5,500 ft (1,675 m). The Dakotas were flying at the highest level. Every 500 ft (150 m) below us another stream of

This is what our Lübeck aerodrome looked like from the control tower. Some of our Dakotas are in view.
(British Berlin Airlift Association)

Second World War SAAF pilots on arrival at Lübeck, very close to the Russian zone, are greeted by an RAF wing commander. (SAAF Museum)

various types of aircraft were joining the twenty-mile (32 km) wide corridor into Berlin. We were carrying parachutes, as it would be impossible for the few aerodromes equipped with GCA (Ground-Controlled Approach) let-down procedures to get us all down in case the mist closed in. Those of us in Dakotas would have to abandon our aircraft and parachute down to earth.

This was the first time I had flown a Dakota without having a second pilot. During take-off my wireless operator sat in the second pilot's seat for the purpose of raising the undercarriage on my command. To raise it myself would mean dropping my head and bending forward to reach down to unlock the undercarriage lever and pull it up. Not a thing to safely do immediately after take-off by the pilot flying the plane!

That first flight to Berlin, and having to be over Franhou Beacon at such an exact time, was difficult. Fortunately we were not in cloud all the way. I called up on my RT 'Over Franhou'. Immediately my message was responded to with the words, 'Turn 90 degrees starboard for identification.' Hardly had I begun my turn when the voice came back, 'I have you identified. Resume course and change frequency for let-down.' I was amazed at the speed of the controller in identifying us on his little radar screen.

Lübeck air traffic control – without their skill and expertise the airlift would have failed. We aircrew owed them a great debt of gratitude.

I had flown Dakotas on the long ten-day flight to Cairo and back to Pretoria many times and loved flying them. On our many, many flights from Lübeck to Berlin, these legendary aircraft performed magnificently.

I flew over a hundred loads of coal to Berlin and returned with many refugees. SAAF aircrew flew in over 16,000 tons of supplies and flew out around 7,000 refugees, in just under 4,000 round trips flown day and night. (British Berlin Airlift Association)

Three minutes ahead of us was another Dakota. As we settled down into our approach pattern for landing I saw his wheels come down and began to feel his slipstream. Immediately after he touched down I saw another Dakota on the ground turn onto the runway for take-off. His tail was up before the plane in front of him that had just landed had cleared the runway. The wheels of my Dakota touched the runway a few seconds after the wheels of the take-off plane had been lifted off.

In good weather conditions there was an aircraft movement on that single runway at Gatow every minute and a half. When the Russians closed all access to Berlin by rail, road and waterways through their occupied territory to Berlin, they never believed that the Allies would be able to fly in supplies in sufficient quantities to keep the two and a half million Berliners alive. They knew that prior to the blockade the Berliners had been supplied with 12,000 tons a day. The Russians also knew that if it came to war, they were in a powerful position. They had 300,000 troops around the city, whereas the Allied garrisons inside had barely 12,000 men.

One day when I was coming in to land, a Skymaster diverted from the American zone aerodrome of Templehof requested landing permission at Gatow. But with Dakotas taking off and landing every one and a half minutes there was no way he could be fitted in. He had to take his fully laden plane back to his base in Western Germany. He must have felt terrible arriving back fully laden.

Tom Condon wins AFC

One of our SAAF pilots, Lt Tom Condon, had an engine failure one night as he was coming in to land at Gatow. Ground control helped him to steer his stricken Dakota through heavy thick clouds and snow. Then suddenly ground control called to say they had lost him on their radar screens. He continued without the help of GCA, but when he broke cloud he found they were just above the runway but too high to land. They were losing height fast and a crash seemed inevitable. There was only one thing that could be done – throw out the sacks of coal. Fortunately his wireless operator was a weight-lifter. With the help of the navigator he hurled sack after sack out of the plane, saving it from crashing. Most of the cargo landed in the Wansee Lake and adjoining forest, but a bag landed on the pantry of General Brian Robertson, the commander of the British Army.

With the heavy load of coal gone, Tom Condon was able to get into Gatow, in the slot of another plane that had to go back with its load for Berlin. For this magnificent effort Tom was awarded the Air Force Cross, and the two other crew members were honourably mentioned.

Some of our SAAF aircrew wait for a Dakota to be made serviceable. We could only fly during a block of time allotted to us and with only three minutes between aircraft. (SAAF Museum)

Our Dakotas that flew in three and a half tons of coal were offloaded in a few minutes and the coal dust was hurriedly swept out and canvas seats fitted under the windows would be lowered for our passengers.

Dakota carried York load?

On one very wet night we climbed into our aircraft and in the dark found our way past all those bags of coal as best we could. On take-off I found this Dakota to be very sluggish. It took longer that usual to get the tail up. Acceleration was poor, too, and it was a struggle to get into the air. Something was obviously wrong, but it wasn't the engines, which were giving their usual power. Perhaps we had been wrongly loaded with a York load instead of a Dakota load. Knowing the phenomenal ability of Dakotas to pull out heavy loads I decided to give it a try. At full power we eventually made it to 5,500 ft (1,675 m), but we were behind time. I decided to see if we could catch up by using almost full power to get to the Fronhau Beacon.

Some of the thousands that we flew out of Berlin. (Berlin Airlift Association)

We counted it a privilege to be able to fly these Germans to a better life in the West. (Berlin Airlift Association)

It was with great relief that we made it on time and did not have to turn back. Fortunately, with bad weather like this, we did not have another aircraft three minutes behind us on our tail. The gap at night in such bad weather was increased to five minutes. I approached for landing with much more power than usual and less flap. The landing felt a bit heavy, but all was well. When we reached our off-loading place and a truck came up to off-load, I left instructions for the number of sacks to be counted and for someone to inform me after our cup of coffee, but when we returned to our aircraft fifteen minutes later, there was no one to be seen.

They had obviously off-loaded and swept out the plane as speedily as possible to make a getaway before our return to avoid telling me the number of sacks of coal, which they knew would then be reported at Lübeck, resulting in their colleagues getting into serious trouble. So I have never been sure if it was a York load that we carried. I think it was, as it happened more than once during the Berlin Airlift. A York load was nine tons; I've heard various figures given for a Dakota load from Lübeck. Three and a half tons is the figure in my brain. Could we really have pulled nine tons? I will never know.

When we landed and taxied to our off-loading points, lorries would be there waiting to off-load and sweep out the dreadful black coal dust. If we were taking back a passenger load of refugees, then the collapsed canvas-covered seats fitted to both sides of the fuselage would be pulled down for use. Meanwhile my crew and I would make our way to a nearby hut for a cup of coffee. Twenty minutes was allowed for off-loading, sweeping and reloading with passengers. When we were carrying passengers, we noticed as we made our way to our cabin past these refugees on either side of us that there was hardly a smile on any face. They looked beaten and were drably dressed in black clothes and there was a faint smell of sauerkraut in the air. We carried our passengers in RAF planes. We, as the South African contingency, did not bring our own Dakotas over from South Africa. The RAF had enough wartime Dakotas left. What they wanted from the Commonwealth was aircrew.

A foolish mistake

As aircrew we operated on a twenty-three-hour day. If we began our day at 7 a.m. one day, the next day it would begin at 6 a.m. and so on. That was not easy on our rhythm of sleep, but we coped. One night around midnight when it was dark and raining heavily, I skimped on my preflight check and on take-off found that my airspeed indicator was not working. 'Oh no, you fool!' I almost shouted at myself. I had forgotten to take off the cover from the airspeed pitot tube, despite the long red warning piece of material attached to it that only a fool could miss. I was in a dilemma. I knew I should really return to base and acknowledge my stupid mistake, losing my time slot to Berlin. Or perhaps I could make it to Berlin and still get to the Fronhau Beacon on time. My pride made me choose that course of action. Fortunately by then I had flown to Gatow more than fifty times and I knew the exact power settings to use. To my delight we made it over Fronhau exactly on time. When I confided to another pilot friend on our return to Lübeck he said, 'Why didn't you turn on the heating switch for the pitot tube for use in icy conditions? That would have burned it off.' 'Ag, ja man,' I responded. 'Why didn't I think of that!'

Later, back in South Africa as a staff-flying instructor on Dakotas at Central Flying School at Dunottar in the Transvaal, I never forgot to remind my pupils – mainly senior officers converting onto Dakotas – the lessons I learned on the Berlin Airlift.

The marvel of GCA

On one occasion, on a return flight to base without any passengers on board because the weather was pretty bad, we were told to divert to Wunstorf because the weather was so atrocious at Lübeck, they couldn't get us down there. Wunstorf had GCA and was on our route. Being at 5,500 ft (1,675 m), there were other aircraft every 500 ft (150 m) below us waiting for their turn to be let down. As I circled and circled, I watched my fuel carefully. We were given enough fuel at Lübeck to take us to Gatow and back, but not much extra. That enabled us to carry the heaviest load of cargo to Berlin as possible. Eventually I called up the control tower and said, 'If you do not give us a priority let-down we will have to bale out and abandon this plane.' We got the priority!

Some of my fellow SAAF pilots on the Berlin Airlift: Major Blaauw with RAF Flying Officer Jenkins in the door-way, Lieutenant Joubert on the steps and Lieutenants Ralston, Delport and Pretorious with Major Barlow.

Despite the many flying hazards and bad weather, we lost comparatively few aircraft. Unfortunately this Dakota came down in Berlin.

BEAUFIGHTER OVER THE BALKANS

I greatly admired those controllers who could work out a route for us to follow from above all the other aircraft and get us down below them safely and onto final approach. By that time my wireless operator was sitting in the second pilot's seat next to me, looking hard through the windscreen ready to shout as soon as he could see the ground. That loud relieved shout only came at about 50 ft (15 m) when he said, 'I can just make out the runway.' We got down all right but had great difficulty in finding a way off the runway in dense mist conditions.

One of our other SAAF pilots was brought down by GCA controllers in even worse conditions. His wireless operator never did see the runway. The first they knew was when they felt the wheels hitting the runway. To think they were able to do that so many years ago is quite something. No wonder it has been said that the heavy cost of the Berlin Airlift was worth every penny because of what we learned about air traffic control in that year of operations. It is quite amazing that we lost so few men and aircraft.

Airlift averted war

By the time the Airlift ended I had flown over 100 loads of coal and other supplies from Lübeck to Gatow and many refugees out to the West. What the exact figure was I do not know, as two and a half years later, after I had resigned my permanent commission with the SAAF to become a missionary pilot in Central Africa, using an old de Havilland Rapide, my number two logbook containing everything about my participation with the Berlin Airlift was burnt when the thatch on our house caught fire. In a few minutes everything my wife, three children and I had, was burned up in that roaring inferno.

We did not fully realise the significance of what we were doing at the time when we were almost routinely flying to Berlin. But in retrospect and after reading much of what has since been written about this amazing feat, I now recognise what a great privilege it was to have been involved in such an historical flying event. Had we failed, the Allies would have been forced to save the two and a half million Berliners from starvation. If they had forced a way through by rail and road, they would not have succeeded with 300,000 Russian troops in the area and only 12,000 Allied troops in the Berlin garrisons. I think hostilities would have been inevitable, leading possibly to a Third World War. This time it would have been against the Russians, who had not wound down their war machine as we in the West had done.

It is good to know that the Berlin Airlift of 1948/9 has not been forgotten. Years later, Helmut Kohl, the Chancellor of the Federal Republic of Germany, and Hans-Dietrich Genscher, the Minister of Foreign Affairs, gave credit to those involved in the 'courageous and spectacular Airlift'. In remembering those who had lost their lives they added, 'The Airlift will not be forgotten'.

One day years later in Ethiopia when I was serving with Mission Aviation Fellowship, I met a German missionary from Berlin. When he heard that I was one of the pilots of the planes he and other children waved at as we came in to land, he enthused, 'I must write home tonight and tell my parents that I've met one of the pilots.'

Russians dumbfounded

Although the Russian barriers went up on the autobahn at Helmstedt on 12 May 1949 at one minute past midnight, and the first convoy of British trucks poured through with supplies for Berlin, the Airlift did not come to an abrupt end. It continued at a reduced rate until 1 August 1949, and after that it was slowly run down, with all aircraft being withdrawn by 1 October.

A total of 689 aircraft had taken part, being 441 American, 147 RAF and 101 British civil aircraft. It is estimated that 124 million miles (almost 200 million kilometres) were flown, airlifting 2,325,808 tons at a cost of about $350,000,000 and the loss of sixty-five lives.

At our former *Luftwaffe* base of Lübeck, one of our RAF Dakotas, KN652, left Lübeck for Gatow at 18.30 hours on 23 September. It bore the inscription:

Positively the last load from Lubeck – 73,705 tons.

Psalm 21: verse 11.

'For they intended evil against thee: they imagined a mischievous device which they are not able to perform.'

Many of us who had not forgotten the miracle of Dunkirk also believed that without God's help we would never have succeeded. The Russians were dumbfounded.

Airlift a miracle

Before returning to South Africa, I was invited, as a member of the Officers' Christian Union, to a meeting at the London flat of General Sir William and Lady Dobbie. He had said, as Governor of Malta when all seemed lost, 'With God's help we will maintain the security of this fortress.' It was a prayer meeting that night. It made me realise that we had not been alone on that Airlift. Back in England, in the Dominions, in America and in Europe, many were praying for a miracle.

One of the most vivid memories of my time on the Berlin Airlift was the one and only time that I was taken into the centre of Berlin. Although the Second World War had been over for more than three years, no pavements could be seen. They were still covered with the rubble of buildings that had been destroyed by the war. I did not see any cars, or many people moving around. It seemed to be a city that would never again be rebuilt,

After Berlin

When the Berlin Airlift came to an end we returned to England and were summoned to South Africa House in London's Trafalgar Square. We were commended for our part in helping to save those two and a half million Western Berliners from starvation and for overcoming and defeating Russia's blockade. It was very satisfying to us all to have been involved in this amazing and historic Airlift, although the full significance of it did not dawn on us immediately.

Two days later we were on our way back to South Africa and to our families, from whom we had been separated for all those months. For me, I not only had the satisfaction of being involved as a pilot on the Berlin Airlift, which I later began to realise was a miracle, but I was also able to see something of the land of my birth. Because I had foreign currency I was able to buy a brand-new car, and was issued petrol coupons for almost unlimited travel during my monthly five-day breaks, which I always spent in England. When I turned up outside the officers' mess at the RAF air station at Bassingbourne, this new car became the centre of attraction. New British cars were mainly at that time for the export trade. Very few new cars were to be seen on British roads. I intended leaving my car out in the open outside the officers' mess during my times at Lübeck. But they would not hear of it, and I was given a garage for it.

This car gave me the opportunity of going as far north as Edinburgh, where I stayed in the home of one of the Associates of the Officers' Christian Union, who were renowned for their prayers. This single lady lived with her father in a large house. I found that her father was one of Scotland's famous sculptors. It was also possible to stay in Southampton with my old friend of Pietersburg days, John Halifax, who was about to be married to Betty. I was able to get them a tea service from Germany, something that was not available in UK. My car had served its purpose, and I passed it over at a reduced price to a friend of my Bible College days, Paul Reid, a British-trained lawyer who had given up his career to go to South Africa to work with the Children's Special Service Mission, heading up that great work throughout the whole of South Africa. He was in urgent need of a good car. So this car that had been so useful to me, met Paul's need.

That car also made it possible for me to see where my Uncle Fred had lived ever since the end of the First World War on a small-holding at Sopley, near Christchurch, where he kept his yacht. He was a great yachtsman and had won many trophies. One of his friends at the club one day told him that the only reason for him winning so many races was that he had the best yacht. So my uncle exchanged yachts with him for the next race and he still won it! He was fourteen years older than my father and I tried to persuade him to accept my father's invitation to go and live on our farm in South Africa. With that plan in mind, I helped him by sorting out his many accumulated belongings.

Berlin forty, and then fifty, years later

My next glimpse of Berlin came nearly forty years later. Kay and I were returning to England from Australia. The Trans-Siberian railway had just been reopened to foreign travellers, so we boarded the Oriental Express at Hong Kong to make our way through China, breaking our journey in

Beijing to visit the Forbidden City, the Great Wall of China and the Ming Tombs, before our further days and nights on the train through Mongolia.

We then travelled three more days and nights through Siberia to Moscow, and from there to Warsaw, where police with Alsatians abruptly ordered us out of our compartment to raise the cover of our seats to make sure that we were not smuggling anyone out of Russia. One police armed guard walked the length of the train on its roof. Others with their sniffer dogs were on the railway line level to make sure no one was hiding under the train. It was an unnerving experience to those of us who were totally unaccustomed to that kind of treatment. When we arrived at East Berlin we saw again armed police with their dogs on the station waiting for us. No one dared get off the train for a few moments to stretch our legs. We could see very little of East Berlin itself. There was no great show of lights. But when our train was on the move again and we crossed the Berlin Wall, the contrast was startling. West Berlin was aglow with sparkling lights. This once great city had indeed risen to its former glory.

Our next experience of Berlin came in 1999. I was among the thousand Berlin Airlift veterans and their wives or near-relatives who were invited to Berlin by the German Airlift Gratitude Foundation for three days of celebrations. It was to commemorate the fiftieth anniversary of the Berlin Airlift victory. The Foundation paid all the air travel expenses to Berlin from New Zealand, Australia, South Africa, America, Canada and the United Kingdom. They also put us up in fine hotels all over Berlin. Coaches were laid on each day to show us the city. We were taken on the waterways, where lunches were served, and also to many special events laid on to honour us.

Kay and I arrived in Berlin a few days beforehand at the invitation of some of the Berlin churches that had invited me to speak in some meetings they arranged, and in Sunday services. Kay also took part in some of them. Before going into our hotel, we had the great privilege of being invited to stay for those few days with a retired American colonel, Eugene Bird, and his lovely Austrian wife, Heidi. As committed Christians we struck up an instant friendship. When Eugene was a youth of nineteen he was in Berlin with the US military forces at the time of the Berlin Airlift. In fact he was the first, or one of the first, Airlift passengers to be flown out of Berlin. He was exuberant in his praises of what we had accomplished.

This is what Eugene wrote for *Beaufighter Over The Balkans*,

'I would like to express my highest regards to the pilots and other airmen of many nations who bravely did their part in supplying all the needs of this great city of Berlin by air transport.

It was shortly after the end of World War II that I arrived in Berlin. My unit was the first to be stationed there.

When we arrived, eighty-five per cent of Berlin lay in ruins. The experts estimated that it would take sixteen years, with three hundred box car loads of rubble a day, just to clear the streets. There

Colonel Eugene Bird was the American Commandant of Spandau prison in Berlin during the last years of Rudolph Hess's life. We discussed Hess at length and his biography of Hess, *The Loneliest Man in the World*, which was translated into twelve languages. Was Hess deliberately murdered? Why? Because he knew too much? If so, by which country?

were very few men in Berlin after the war, however, the 'Berlin Rubble Women' cleared the streets much sooner than expected and 'West Berlin' became a 'Show Case of Freedom'. It became a thriving, industrial city, which was a 'thorn in the eye' to Joseph Stalin and the Soviet Union.

To hinder the re-birth of 'West Berlin', the Soviets harassed where they could, such as blocking or delaying trains coming in or out. Or breaking the sound barrier over Berlin. Or threatening to blockade the city, which they later did.

At the time of the blockade, we were on 'high alert', fully armed, but we were only one battalion of 1,000 men and only twelve armoured vehicles. We were no match for 360,000 Russian troops together with their 3,500 tanks that surrounded the city. Nevertheless we were ready with the British and French to do our part in attempting to defend the city because of the importance of West Berlin to the free world, both economically and strategically.

We were told at the time, that US planes were flying around the area of Wiesbaden, loaded with atomic bombs, waiting for orders to attack. This was the start of the Berlin blockade, which resulted in the Air Lift. A plane landed on one of our three airports in Berlin every sixty seconds, bringing in food and supplies to feed the city of over three million people.

I still love Berlin, having been here for fifty years. In my later years, I served as US Director of Spandau Allied Prison, which housed the major war criminals, who were tried and sentenced during the Nuremburg War Criminal Trials. I wrote a book together with Rudolph Hess, the deputy to Adolph Hitler, which became a bestseller and went into twelve countries. In England it was called, 'The Loneliest Man In The World – The Life Story of Rudolph Hess'.'

At one time Eugene was the Commandant of the famous Spandau prison where Rudolph Hess was held for all those years. Eugene wrote the best-selling biography of Hess that went into twelve languages. He has strong evidence to refute the notions that Hess committed suicide by hanging himself, because at that age he could not possibly raise his arms to place the noose around his neck. He also dismissed the idea that it was not actually Rudolf Hess that died.

He and Heidi drove us all over Berlin to show us all the main historic sights, including what

Spandau Prison – why, as a very old man, and the only one left in Spandau Prison, was Hess not released?

remains of the Berlin Wall. The contrast of that bustling city to what I had seen of rubblefilled empty streets fifty years before was aweinspiring.

Eugene also took us to meet another American who had also become a permanent resident of Berlin. He was Captain Jack Bennett, who had flown more loads of supplies to Berlin on the Berlin Airlift than any other man. He gave me an autographed edition of the little booklet he and Andreas Anderhub had written, 'Blockade, Airlift and Airlift Gratitude Foundation – Concerning the History of the Berlin Crisis 1948-49'.

Jack had flown 1,000 loads of supplies to Berlin, which made my total of just over a hundred seem as nothing. He must have had many hair-raising experiences. I wish he had written about them. But being a modest man, it is not something he would write about. It is too late now. He died a few years ago and now Eugene has since died. Time for me in my late 80s must also be running out:

It was on the evening of 23rd June 1948 when he was with the American Overseas Airline (later called Panam) at Frankfurt Airport that he received a phone call from the US Air Force base on the other side of the airfield. He did not recognise the voice at the time, but it turned out to be General Lucius Clay, the main architect of what became known as 'The Berlin Airlift'. The conversation went like this:

Captain Jack Bennett, who I met in Berlin during the 50th Berlin Airlift celebrations in Berlin in 1999. He flew 1,000 loads of supplies to Berlin during the blockade. This war more than any other Berlin Airlift pilot.

'Captain, do you have a DC-4 airplane to fly coal to Berlin?'

Jack Bennett wrote in his booklet:

'My feet came off my desk to the floor with a bang. I responded with "You're kidding! Coal dust would ruin our passenger cabins. We're carrying people on our airline. Doesn't the Air Force have freighters over there?"

'General Clay responded to that by saying, "No, surprisingly, we don't! We have only two DC-4's in Europe and they are not in Germany".'

This photo was taken by Captain Bennett of a Soviet MiG fighter. They would usually harass Berlin Airlift planes close to Berlin.

The Soviets had been playing cat and mouse with the autobahns, trains, and waterways into Berlin, shutting them down for hours at a time. But on this day, the 23rd June 1948 Helmstedt had been closed all day. General Clay told Jack Bennett that Intelligence had informed them that this time it might be permanent. And that it might mean having to supply Berlin by air. Having heard Jack's reaction to carrying coal he said, "How about flying potatoes in sacks". Jack responded, "Well I suppose I can. How soon can you sack the potatoes?" The General replied, "By say 8.00pm. You might be making history. Your trip is the first in what might be a long blockade of Berlin."

And so it was. Jack Bennett flew that first load of supplies to Berlin that night.

At 6.00am the following morning, the Soviets officially and totally severed all traffic to and from Berlin. General Clay described this as, 'one of the most ruthless efforts in modern times to use mass starvation for political coercion'.

After Jack's first flight of the airlift, his evening flights continued to Berlin until 26th June, when the USAF officially implemented the airlift with a few aircraft of their own. It was not until almost two months later that the USA Army Force planes arrived.

Four days after the USAF officially began the airlift, on 30 June 1948, the British Foreign Secretary, Ernest Bevin announced that the British would participate in the airlift and for a start DC3s would be used because they were readily available.

When Eugene Bird took Kay and I to meet Jack Bennett I had no idea that we would be meeting such a famous pilot and the most renowned Berlin Airlift pilot. On that Berlin Airlift operation of 462 days, he had flown almost every day, including the first day and the last. After the Berlin Airlift he became Chief Pilot of PanAm Europa and was awarded the Federal Service Cross.

Jack and his German wife lived in a beautiful home in a lovely leafy suburb of Berlin not far from where Eugene and his young and beautiful Austrian wife lived. His large home had a most elegant broad central stairway leading to the upper floor. It was, to Kay and to me, reminescent of many of the staircases in British stately homes. The garden was huge, leading down a slope to a wonderfully picturesque lake, where he had a lovely wooden garden hut to relax in and watch the birdlife on the lake.

From then on Eugene and Jack began to see much more of each other. Perhaps because Eugene and Heidi had entertained a Berlin Airlift pilot in their home. Eugene having married first a German wife who died after a long illness and then married Heidi, meant that he was most fluent in German, which had become their home language. He was in constant demand as a speaker, not only in Berlin but also much farther afield. Sometimes Jack would go and hear him speak or preach. Before he died, Jack became a committed Christian.

During our couple of days with Eugene it soon became apparent to me how well known he was. At the Tempelhof memorial service and laying of wreaths, which included one from the South African Air Force, with flags from the various countries involved with the Berlin Airlift blowing in the breeze, Eugene seemed to know everyone of importance. He seemed to be greeting everyone, and introduced me to a number of them, including the Mayor of Berlin, to whom I gave one of the thousand 'Berlin Airlift Miracle' pamphlets I had written to remind everyone that the triumph of the Berlin Airlift was not just because of us, but God's hand upon the venture.

Just as I had not known what a famous man Jack Bennett was when I met him, I did not know how outstanding a man Eugene was, until years later when Heidi, after his death, sent me information I had requested.

Eugene Bird was of British descent and had been able to trace his family back to 1260 and Cambridgeshire. His ancestors went to America in the 1700s to Virginia. He grew up on a farm where life was far from easy with constant droughts. His future became focused by being given a book about American presidents which he read over and over again. It made him ponder on the lives of great men of history. He vowed to join their ranks.

At eighteen, he was drafted into the US Army during World War II, where he fought as an infantryman in three campaigns in the European theatre of operations. He was the 7th man to spearhead the crossing of the bridge of Remagen in Germany and was decorated with the Bronze Star for Bravery. General Eisenhower was later to remark that the capture of the Remagen Bridge was 'worth its weight in gold' as it shortened the war by some months.

In 1951 he was assigned to the United Nations Command in Korea, where as an Infantry (tactical and technical) advisor to some twenty-two nations of the United Nations Command, he was presented by the King of Thailand with 'the Most Honorable Order of the Crown of Thailand' in recognition of his service to the Thai Army.

After his book about Hess took off in so many countries, he became well known internationally and went on to help produce eighteen films. He became the only person in the world to appear on the US CBS television programme '60 minutes' three times. In Germany, he helped produce a serial entitled, 'Augenzeugenberichte'.

Eugene had a strong personal commitment to furthering human rights causes through human rights and charitable organisations and was the president of the Berlin section of the Full Gospel Businessman's Association.

What a man! Those couple of days in 1999 in his home and at the various celebrations, established a lasting friendship with him until his death, and continues with Heidi.

Psalm 91

While Kay and I were with Eugene and Heidi, the matter of the Psalm 91st came up because I had spoken about it in meetings and in a half-hour interview for German television. I told my German audiences that I believed that my life in the Second World War, and indeed on the Berlin Airlift, was saved because of the special prayers of my parents and their claiming the promises of that psalm of protection. Eugene Bird told me what he knew of Psalm 91 in the First World War in the Somme when losses of men of the Allied force were extremely high. One American brigade who were given copies of Psalm 91 were asked to keep it on them and to read it and claim the promises in that psalm every morning. Colonel Bird said that Congressional records show that while losses in other brigades were high, not one man in that brigade died due to enemy action. How I wish I had known of this during my time in Italy during the Second World War. I would have encouraged our Padre to do the same with all our squadrons at Biferno, including the Italian squadron and then hopefully throughout the Balkan Air Force and even beyond that. Maybe, Captain Dickson – 'Dickie' – would not have died when his Beaufighter was shot down close to Cernik Castle. The photo taken of the crash showed that the wings were broken off and smashed up so much that they were not identifiable in the photo. But amazingly the main part of the fuselage was intact.

The Partisans who had asked us to attack Cernik Castle on that day saw the crash and rushed down from their vantage point on a hill and found that Dickie was dead but his navigator was alive and only sustained a black eye. I wondered if he had been praying and because he had believing parents back at home. If only I had done in the Second World War what was done in the Somme in the First. Here is Psalm 91 in a modern translation, using words that express the meaning of the words

BEAUFIGHTER OVER THE BALKANS

in the English language of today:

> You who sit down in the High God's presence, spend the night in Shaddai's shadow,
> Say this: 'GOD, you're my refuge; I trust in you and I'm safe!'
> That's right – he rescues you from hidden traps, shields you from deadly hazards.
> His huge outstretched arms protect you – under them you're perfectly safe; his arms fend off all harm.
> Fear nothing – not wild wolves in the night, not flying arrows in the day,
> Not disease that prowls through the darkness, not disaster that erupts at high noon. Even though others succumb all around, drop like flies right and left, no harm will even graze you.
> You'll stand untouched, watch it all from a distance, watch the wicked turn into corpses.
> Yes, because God's your refuge, the High God your very own home.
> Evil can't get close to you, harm can't get through the door.
> He ordered his angels to guard you wherever you go.
> If you stumble, they'll catch you; their job is to keep you from falling.
> You'll walk unharmed among lions and snakes,
> and kick young lions and serpents from the path.
> 'If you'll hold on to me for dear life,' says GOD, 'I'll get you out of any trouble. I'll give you the best of care if you'll only get to know and trust me.
> Call me and I'll answer, be at your side in bad times; I'll rescue you,
> then throw you a party. I'll give you a long life,
> give you a long drink of salvation!'

Epilogue

It was hoped that the First World War would be the war to end all wars. Yet within a quarter of a century, the Second World War commenced and millions died as a result of this bloody conflict. Hiroshima and Nagasaki were destroyed by what Leonard Cheshire saw as a 'tiny' nuclear device in comparison to the possibilities of the future, when the planet with all mankind could be annihilated. It was again hoped that the Second World War would be the war to end all wars. So many countries have, as Cheshire predicted, nuclear armaments. There is now such a fear that some madman will use them that wars seem to be inevitable. One wonders what the twenty-first century holds for mankind, and indeed our wonderful planet.

Modern warfare is becoming more and more detached from reality. In my ten years as a pilot with the South African Air Force, I never saw a dead body in close-up. And yet I must have killed many people with my four 20 mm cannons and eight rockets. At the time when I looked at the photos of my attacks, I always felt gratified when I saw that I had successfully destroyed a target. Today I look at those photos in a different way. I think of the people who must have been in those buildings alive and well one moment and then, when I pressed the button, were dead or horrifically injured. The Japanese called the Beaus 'whispering death', because our engines were so quiet. I long for the day when 'swords will be turned into ploughshares', as the Bible puts it, and 'death will be no more'.

When I was coming to an end of writing my autobiography of *Beaufighter Over the Balkans* and also *From War to Peace*, it struck me that those who might read my book about war, might not read my book about peace, a book about showing how 'weapons of war' became 'tools of peace'.

While I was pondering how to end the book so that the reader might realise that there is a brighter side to flying than destruction and killing, an Italian newspaper called *Nuovo Molise* was sent to me by Guiseppe Morini, who lives in Campomarino, close to where our Second World War airfield at Biferno used to be. He has been devoting a great deal of time and effort into researching what the Balkan Air Force did from the five airfields in his area. He tracked down my name and address. I sent him my six Balkan Air Force aviation magazine articles, as well as what appeared in Peter Bagshawe's book, *Passion for Flight*. During the past year many letters and phone calls have passed between us.

Then his wife, Margherita, a teacher, wrote an article and sent it to this widely read newspaper, which to her surprise published it in full at the very time when her husband was making a presentation of what had taken place at Biferno all those years ago to the Mayor, Councillors and the people of Campomarino. The English teacher in her school translated it into English so that I could read what appeared with two photos in this Italian paper.

It seems appropriate to me to end with Margherita's article so that readers of this book might catch a glimpse of what I've also written about in *From War to Peace*. Margherita also touches on my fight against 'degrading social values'. Kay and I have been engaged in a war against the cultural collapse in the Western world. My third book is about the Festival of Light that we helped to found in 1971. As I write, I fear for Britain. The latest terrorism attack in London went off at half-cock. There could well be another as devastating as the Twin Towers attack. Our cultural collapse in the West could well be one of the reasons for terrorism.

STEVE STEVENS DFC
A story of war and peace
of a Beaufighter rocket-firing pilot
during the Second World War in Campomarino

Campomarino, 9 June 2003
Written by Dott.ssa Margherita Recchia

There are two ways to interpret history. The first being that which we live each day in the things we do for ourselves and for others. Then there's the second, which comes alive in heroic actions worthy of mention in history books. The following story encompasses both of these visions and tells the tale of a man, first an airman and then a missionary pilot, who gives and continues to give his life to humanity. A unique story of its kind, that changed the fate and destiny of many, both in times of war and peace. This is the right definition for Steve Stevens, a pilot in the South African Air Force during the Second World War in Campomarino (1944–45). A man divided between war and peace who, as a Christian, decided to take a stand when life imposed difficult and important choices for the good of many. A wonderful story which intertwined with that of our land, the city of Campomarino during the Second World War. A man of great human and military virtues, he was decorated with the Distinguished Flying Cross.

Margherita went on to recount my early life on the farm in South Africa and the impact my father's conversion to Christianity had on us all.

This marked the beginning of a beautiful adventure for Steve that would last him a lifetime. When the war broke out on the world scene, he was at Cape Town at the South African Biblical Institute. Because he was a Christian, he had to be ready to serve his country knowing that the lives of many, including his, were on the line. In 1941 Steve begins his career as a young pilot and after a brief period of time, he becomes a flight instructor for three years until 1944 when he is sent to English flight training camps near Cairo.

Steve begins his adventure with the Beaufighters of the 19th Squadron of the South African Air Force, constituted in Campomarino at the Biferno airfield. He continued to fly these planes until the end of the war. Many were the missions that took off from Campomarino, among these there are two which are especially remembered for their outcome, for their audacity and for their danger: the attack on the SS *Kuckuck* armed ship in the port of Fiume and the attack on Cernick Castle, a German headquarters where orders to the troops were dispatched. After Campomarino and the end of the war in Europe, there was the possibility Steve could have been sent to the Orient, as Japan had decided to continue the war and not surrender. But the international situation underwent a drastic change following the drop of the atomic bomb on Hiroshima and Nagasaki, which put an end to the Second World War.

This disastrous event changed the concept of war, which lost its sense of values and became an image of destruction of things and above all, of people. The new image of war was unacceptable to Steve, even if he continued to fly as a military pilot up until 1950, he started to look towards his future in a different way. At the end of the war, he marries Kay who gives him three children. Kay is a strong woman with whom he'll share the rest of his life and stand by her, sharing fully the events that will impose important and courageous choices. In the meantime, Steve takes part in numerous military peace missions. Among these are two historic missions in which the South African Air Force took part and where Steve participated in all respect as an expert military pilot, showing his duty, love, passion and dedication as this important moment required of him when the destiny of entire populations was on the line. One of the humanitarian missions, the Berlin Airlift (the first signs of the Cold War), takes place outside the African continent. It helped Berliners who were dying of hunger because of the Russian embargo on Berlin at the end of the Second World War.

Steve and other Anglo-American pilots went on numerous missions continually for about a year, carrying in aids of primary necessity to the Berliners. The other mission helped the South African country against the tsetse fly that was killing off a good part of Zulu's cattle herds. One day, during one of his numerous transport flights for military delegations, Steve finds himself in the city of Khartoum and he is invited to tea at the Sudan Interior Mission. The missionaries tell him of their difficulties in working on the Sudanese territory because of the heavy rains which for many months every year would impede them from bringing help to the numerous villages and tribes as the territory's fragile network of communication would become impossible. The solution, as the missionaries pointed out, should have come from the sky, as an aeroplane would have alleviated the suffering of many people. The missionaries' words fill Steve's heart and touch him profoundly.

BEAUFIGHTER OVER THE BALKANS

These words are for Steve an unmistakable sign of how his life should change. Upon his return to South Africa, Steve receives a letter from his father telling him that a new charity organization, the Mission Aviation Fellowship (MAF), was attempting to create an aviation unit for missions. Steve, at this point, has no doubts; this is the way God wants him to take. He immediately gets in contact with the new organization which was seeking out funds to buy a small plane. The missions would have started later on, so Steve continued to fly for the military air force for a couple of years, going on then to join the Mission Aviation Fellowship (MAF) organization. During his time on the 'Berlin Airlift', he visits the new MAF organization in London. Here he is told that he will be the first missionary pilot for the MAF in Africa and that he will be working in Sudan but not before he obtains a senior civil flying permit. He will obtain the permit paying out of his own pocket and will also face the costs of getting to the Sudan with his family. The new organization had directed all of its funds towards the purchase of a plane and with great sacrifice was able to sustain the entire organization.

This economic condition characterized the entire period for which Steve belonged to the organization so he never received any pay except for the joy of giving himself to others and to the love of Christ. This economic condition permitted Steve and his family to live a dignified life, but nothing more.

Thus, this young South African pilot decorated with the DFC, abandons a brilliant career which might have taken him to the highest of military ranks and, along with his family, departs to help the missionaries in Africa. He puts his experience to good use to plan and organize an operative aviation unit able to transport aid to the missionaries and to the populations in the most desperate areas of Africa. With great joy, he sees the birth of the first airfields in the immense African landscape and together with the engineer and wireless operator Stuart King, an ex-officer of the RAF, flies thousands of kilometres in a small plane to help entire tribes deep in remote areas where no land vehicle could hardly ever get to, especially when rains would isolate entire areas from the rest of the world.

In this adventure, Steve had both his wife and three children by his side. They lived this difficult life of missions with apprehension and difficulty while being hosted by the missionaries in Africa.

After a few years, Steve starts to have problems with his right eye. The doctors he consults diagnose him with a probable detached retina and only an operation can avoid further complications. His civil flying permit lapsed and Steve faces a painful period because he can't fly for the mission anymore. Steve asks for the help of an old war buddy, Gordon Marshall, also a Christian. His friend's response is immediate and generous and after a brief period of training on the small plane, he becomes operative together with Stuart. Little does Steve know that this adventure will take him on a new road God has in store for him helping others. Steve and his family move to London for a brief period of rest and reflection asking God which road to take.

These questions are quickly answered when he is nominated director of the MAF, a role he will have for seventeen years. During this period of time, the organization will grow in many parts of the world. Steve will see the construction of new landing strips in the most unthinkable parts of the world thanks to his dedication and that of others like him. Today the MAF is present in thirty countries of the world with nearly 130 aeroplanes. Africa, Mongolia, New Guinea, Central and South America are only a few of the continents and the countries where every year goods such as medicine, primary food aids and the sick and doctors are transported for the missions to help the needy populations. Kay and Steve are today honorary members of the Mission Aviation Fellowship in West Sussex. Both are continually active and ready to sustain the organization in its various initiatives, like the one in 1999 where they rallied for funds destined to buy a Cessna for the mission in Mongolia. Today Steve and Kay, faced with degrading social values, are on their country's front line to battle until this society understands that it needs an identity based on Christian values. Numerous are their initiatives against drugs, sex, blasphemous slander, violence and profanity.

They have also, at times, reproved television on programmes for their indecent moral content. With the Iraq international situation, Steve did not hesitate, even for a moment, on which side to stand. He is for a solution against war and for peace. As an Anglo-American Allied pilot during the Second World War, but above all as a Christian, he let himself be heard, sending letters to the President of the United States of America and to some European presidents as well as to numerous newspapers promoting a line of dialogue where peace prevails always over war. The memories of Campomarino are those of the Biferno airfield, of the briefing in the Nissen Hut, the missions over Yugoslavia, the memories of his colleagues, both those living and those gone on to a better life, the nights before the missions in a tent studying maps and reading Psalm 91 from the little bible his father had given him before leaving for the war and training at the firing range at the mouth of the Biferno river. Giuseppe Morini has found Steve in England, he was searching for the history of Allied aviation at Campomarino and along with the war planes he discovered peace planes transporting love. In so doing he has given us Steve's story who spent his life liberating people from the slavery of Nazism and from hunger, both in times of war and peace.

* * *

A recent photo of the author of *Beaufighter Over The Balkans*, Steve Stevens DFC. He is seen with the famous photo of his rocket-firing attack on the Nazi-held medieval fortress town of Zuzemberk in what was then Yugoslavia, on 13 February 1945.

ITALY, 2005
The 60th Anniversary of the end of the Second World War
It is estimated that 55,000,000 died in the Second World War

A few years ago, to my surprise, a letter arrived from Italy. It came from near the small, ancient town of Termoli, halfway up the Adriatic coast and close to the Biferno river, where I had been based in the war. The letter was from Guiseppe Morini, a man half my age but nevertheless a man determined to keep alive the memory of what Allied airmen had done for the Italian people all those years ago.

He wrote to tell me he had read some Balkan Air Force articles I had written for some British aviation magazines.

Guiseppe wanted Kay and me to visit him and his wife Margherita to help him establish exactly where my No. 19 SAAF Beaufighter Squadron was based. He had been able to locate sites for squadrons of fighters, light bombers and No. 16 SAAF rocket-firing Beaufighters, but not No.19.

Because of circumstances at the time, the visit was not possible, although we stayed in contact through letters and phone calls. However, early in 2005 Guiseppe attempted the difficult task of contacting the Italian airmen who were based in Termoli, and the even more difficult task of tracing those from Australia, New Zealand, South Africa, America, Canada, Britain and other European countries. Many survivors of those war years had either died or were suffering from illnesses associated with old age.

Despite Kay being unfit to travel and my continuing pain resulting from shingles, I felt I should make the effort to go. Fortunately the organisation HEROES RETURN provided a grant for myself and a carer. My friend John Ray agreed to come with his camera equipment.

I rang the South African High Commission to find out if any other South African Air Force airmen were planning to also visit Italy and found that none were. On speaking to Colonel Johaan du Plessis, the Military Adviser, he told me he had been looking for a South African Second World War veteran who could attend some of the British VE Day events in Britain.

Guiseppe asked those of us planning to join him to contact the press in our countries, and the *Sunday Mirror* responded to my approach. They sent a photographer to visit me and he was delighted with the quality of the photos that had been taken from the noses of our Beaufighters all those years ago. He was followed by a journalist, and the result was a double-page spread in a newspaper with a weekly circulation of 1,688,000.

Despite all of Guiseppe's hard work, there were only eight of us who eventually made it back to Italy. We were given the warmest of welcomes and invited to share our experiences of sixty years ago.

187

These Italian Air Force Second World War airmen had fought on both sides. Some had been shot down by us before Italy changed sides. Some of them were highly decorated men. When I was flying from the Termoli airstrip in 1944/5, they seemed to suffer more losses of their Baltimores and aircrew than any of our other squadrons. We honoured them for their bravery.

When we, Second World War airmen who had flown from Termoli in 1944/5 were presented with these VE Day commemoration plaques, I told them I would value this as much as my DFC because it was a plaque of PEACE. A woman hears the drone of a plane and is in fear of being bombed yet again. But as she looks up she sees it is a PLANE OF PEACE. That's just what I, and my wife Kay, became involved in Africa with our Mission Aviation Fellowship planes.

Guiseppe Morini, without whom there would have been no VE Day celebrations in Italy, points to, the photo I had presented to the Mayor. On the left is John Chapman, who came as my carer and has also helped considerably with this book. (John Ray)

I presented the Mayor of Campomarino with a framed copy of the famous photo of my Beaufighter rocket attack on the ancient town of Zuzemberk.

The warm-hearted Italians responded most generously, and as I put it later to our local newspaper, I'd never been kissed by so many women – and men!

The climax came on 8 May, the 60th Anniversary of VE Day. The ceremonies were in the open air, with a military band, rousing speeches, and a fly-past. Dignitaries from all over Italy were present, while huge flags of all participating countries blew in the wind. The chief of the Italian Air Force, General Leonardo Tricario, was there and a fifty-strong guard of honour marched into the square in our honour. The Italian Air Force also brought in another fifty men – bandsmen who played rousing music.

Here are extracts from the speech given by the Chief of the Italian Air Force, General Leonardo Tricario.

Here I am, second from right, second row, with RAF and USAAF airmen who had been invited by the Italians to return sixty years later for their VE Day celebrations.

This huge display in the centre of Termoli shows what our PSP runways looked like. Termoli overlooked the Biferno river and it was down there that our runway ran along the sea shore.

Dignitaries, kind guests, citizens of Campomarino I wish before all else to thank the Honourable Undersecretary for the Defense Filippo BERSELLI for having honoured us with his authoritative presence which confers extra solemnity to today's ceremony. My grateful thought also to the Mayor of Campomarino the most courteous Professor Anita DI GIUSEPPE who together with all the members of the citizens Committee has made herself the promoter of such an important and worthy initiative. On behalf of the Air Force, I express the warmest greetings to all those who today, like myself, have the possibility of sharing the emotion and profound significance of this celebration.

Today, however, I have been able to relish the profound emotional intensity which has flowed so genuine and strong from the testimony of an aviator who every time he returns to these places evokes unchanged and lasting the memory of those dramatic days.

Others also, and sadly not a few, from those precarious runway metal strips in the middle of fields took off for the last flight, the highest, towards the shining blue which from that time crowns their pure heroism.

To their memory I address the most grateful and deferential homage.

Still today we draw from their example, a proud motive of being and a vigorous incentive to face the challenges which engage us daily, wherever our intervention is required, for the safety of the Country and for the protection of peace and international stability.

This is a mission which no longer has any limits of latitude or of boundaries. It also includes research operations and aid in the transport of the seriously ill and organs required for immediate transplant operations and which, as shown during the Tsunami in Asia is leaning toward humanitarian action which is ever more participating and widspread and which doesn't allow any exceptions in order to assist those who suffer.

Thank you, with all my heart, for what you have done for Italy, and for the Air Force, for that Armed Forces the whole of which I represent at this moment and which makes us proud today as it did then.

After the presentation of plaques, we all walked to the war memorial to lay wreaths.

The remainder of that last memorable day was taken up with visiting more of the places, where sixty years earlier, metal runways had been laid on fields where the countryside was flat enough for runways.

The United States Air Force pilots who had come over for this momentous occasion told us that they had flown Mustangs from one of the sites. They said they had been fitted with extra fuel tanks to enable them to fly to Berlin and back without refuelling – an amazing round-trip distance of around 2,500 miles (4,000 km) for a single-engined fighter.

BEAUFIGHTER OVER THE BALKANS

At another site, Ted Brister, an RAF pilot from the UK flying Spitfires, told us they often had to taxi over muddy ground to reach their metal runway. To prevent a nose-over when using high revs to get out of the mud, two mechanics would sit on either side of the tail plane and scramble off when the Spitfire wheels reached the metal. On one occasion, one of the mechanics waited too long, and when the engine roared into life, the airflow held him there. As the plane took off all he could do was squeeze up as close as he could to the fin and hold on as best he could.

The pilot meanwhile had felt on take-off that something was radically wrong with his Spitfire. Once in the air he looked around and could hardly believe his eyes when he saw his mechanic holding on for dear life! He eased back on the power, but not too much, because it was the airflow that was helping to keep this terrified man in place. Flying very carefully, he made a gentle circuit and got his mechanic down safely. The CO jokingly offered the

With Ted Brister who was here 60 years ago, as a Spitfire pilot with the RAF Desert Air Force Squadron No. 92 – RAF top scoring fighter squadron in the WWII. (Photo: John Ray)

Ted told us of their mechanic who did not jump off the tail plane of the Spitfire in time and was taken up into the air. (Photo: Ted Brister)

mechanic a fiver to do it again, to which he responded, 'Not for a hundred pounds!'

With difficulty Giuseppe and I were eventually able to identify where No. 19 SAAF Beaufighter Squadron had camped. It had been completely built over with new housing, but the terrain was the same.

I felt very privileged to have been invited as a VIP to the only 60th VE Day celebration in Italy, and returned home with wonderful memories, as well as the four hours of video film and over 300 colour photos that John Ray took.

UNITED KINGDOM

My first VE Day invitation in the UK was to be one of eleven invited veterans to take part in the Brookwood Cemetery Commemorative Day, on 26 June.

Representatives and veterans of various branches of the armed forces were there to speak to large numbers of children from local schools. We were to meet with them in small groups to chat with them and answer any questions.

As I spoke to the children I reminded them that the average age of those buried in the cemetery was only just over twenty. Not all were killed outright, some had died later of horrific wounds.

As I was driven away from Brookwood Military Cemetery, I was left with a deep sense of gratitude to the Commonwealth Graves Commission for keeping that wonderful area, and those 5,000 war graves, in such magnificent shape.

MEETING PRINCE CHARLES

My next invitation came from the BBC to attend a function at the Imperial War Museum in London. There were to be no speeches, but the Prince of Wales had been invited to speak informally to the veterans and their guests, while the television cameras rolled. I took my daughter Pam, as my wife was not well enough to accompany me.

When I was introduced to Prince Charles, and after some words together, I mentioned that he and Pam were born at the same time. He joked that she had worn better than he had, and invited her to take a photo of us together. Although she had been told the BBC did not want any private photography, Pam could not refuse the Prince!

I showed Prince Charles the Plaque of Peace I had been presented with in Italy on VE Day, and presented him with a copy of our Mission Aviation Fellowship book, *Hope has Wings*. Minutes later the Prince's equerry, Richard Pattle, an RAF wing commander, introduced himself. He asked if I had known a South African relative of his called Pat Pattle, who had been a famous Second World War pilot.

It so happened that Pat Pattle and I had both been written about in a book about fourteen

Twenty-six Second World War veterans of different Allied nationalities were invited by BBC TV to meet HRH Prince Charles in the board room of the Imperial War Museum on 29 June 2005. The BBC interviewed me and the recording was used as part of the Armistice programme. I was asked what motivated me as a South African to volunteer for war service. My response was 'A just cause and Churchill's stirring speeches'.

South African airmen called *Passion for Flight*. I am now the sole survivor.

A few days later I received a letter from wing commander Richard Pattle:

Dear Steve,

The Prince of Wales has asked me to thank you for your kind gift of the book Hope has Wings *together with the quite extraordinary photograph of your Beaufighter attacking Zuzemberk in 1945. His Royal Highness was very touched by your generosity and enjoyed meeting you. This letter comes with His Royal Highness's best wishes.*

VETERANS AWARENESS WEEK

Many events took place between 4 and 10 July 2005 to celebrate the 60th Anniversary of the end of the Second World War. It was the nation's first Veterans Awareness Week, with Sunday 10 July being National Commemoration Day.

The day began with a Service of Thanksgiving at Westminster Abbey, followed by lunch in the grounds of Buckingham Palace for invited veterans from the armed forces and the home front.

I was invited to attend the Commemorative Event of Reflection and Reminiscence at Horse Guards Parade that afternoon. What I enjoyed very much was the vintage aircraft fly-past, when the skies above London were filled with the formation of Second World War aircraft. They flew over Horse Guards Parade, down the Mall and over Buckingham Palace, in five sections of aircraft spaced at two-minute intervals, and at the approximate height of 1,000 ft (300 m).

It was a thrill for me to see that I had flown three of them – a Spitfire, an Avro Anson, and the Douglas DC-3 Dakota. And then there was the Lancaster – the plane I had been due to fly in the Japanese theatre of war had the dropping of the atom bomb not brought an abrupt end to the war.

The Lancaster that flew over our heads that day was a PA 474, one of only two of the 7,377 that had been built still in an airworthy condition. It performed the crowning ceremony of dropping one million poppies.

I said to Prince Charles, 'I have had reason to think of you ever since you were born' and pointing to Pam continued 'My daughter was born at that same time'. As he shook her hand he remarked, 'You have worn much better than I have!' (Pam Stevens)

In the Garden of Remembrance of Westminster Abbey. Thousands of little wooden crosses had been pressed into the grass plots remember those who had given their lives.

With Colonel Johaan Du Plessis, the military adviser for the South African High Commission in London at Westminster Abbey before the Queen's arrival.

I am on the extreme right with South African servicemen at the Horse Guards Parade prior to the 60th Anniversary of Armistice Day march-past. (Pam Stevens)

The memory of that fly-past will be for ever imprinted on my mind, because when the memory has faded, I will still have the book *Thanks for our Future* that we were given. Inside are four pages of perfectly illustrated details of those vintage planes.

As I now look back on that time of Reflection and Reminiscence, the one thing that has moved me more deeply than anything else is a moving poem, written in 1966 by a twelve-year-old girl.

WHO ARE THESE MEN?

Who are these men who march so proud,
Who quietly weep, eyes closed, head bowed?
These are the men who once were boys,
Who missed out on youth and all its joys.

Who are these men with aged faces,
Who silently count the empty spaces?
These are the men who gave their all,
Who fought for their country, for freedom, for all.

Who are these men with sorrowful look,
Who can still remember the lives that were took?
These are the men who saw young men die,
The price of peace is always high.

Who are these men who in the midst of pain,
Whispered comfort to those they would not see again?
These are the men whose hands held tomorrow,
Who bought back our future with blood, tears and sorrow.

Who are these men who promise to keep
Alive in their hearts the ones God holds asleep?
These are the men to whom I promise again:
Veterans, my friends, I will remember them.

Anonymous twelve-year-old girl 1966

A Beaufighter, but no nose camera in this one. (Photo: Pam Stevens)

It was these rockets with 20 pound solid steel warheads that enabled us to Sink the SS *Kuckuck.* (Photo: Pam Stevens)

These are the rockets that we usually used, with 60 pound explosive warheads. With this larger and heavier warhead we had to fly and aim very accurately to hit a target exactly where we wanted it to hit in the heat of battle. On a firing range I could usually hit an empty 44 gallon fuel barrell. (Photo: Pam Stevens

Appendix

From War to Peace

A flying sequel to *Beaufighter Over the Balkans*

The title has been chosen because the founders and early pioneers of a new flying organisation that was formed as WWII came to a close, were mostly pilots and a few aircraft engineers who were WWII men – and one woman. They had served in the Air Forces of Britain, the United States of America, Australia, New Zealand and South Africa. Only one from South Africa, and that was me.

This book, *From War to Peace*, is mainly an autobiographical account of my becoming Mission Aviation Fellowship's first pilot in Africa in 1950 in an old eight-seater, wood and fabric bi-plane, a de Haviland Rapide. I helped lay the foundations of what is today a highly sophisticated air service that is often dubbed 'God's Airline' with 130 modern aircraft. There was a time when MAF operated nearly 200 aircraft, but with bush and jungle airstrips having been improved most of our small aircraft have been replaced by larger planes. Now we are able to reach out into other countries from some of our main bases.

This book, being autobiographical, concentrates on my story of how, in 1946 when in Khartoum, I was challenged by the need of cut-off missionaries in the remote South Sudan. It was not until 1950 that I made it back to the Sudan. The Government did not want us to fly to places where no other plane had gone before. They demanded that the pilot should have the highest flying qualifications. Fortunately, I was a Staff Flying Instructor at the SAAF Central Flying School at that time, and was able to study and write my flying exams in only six weeks. I was, I believe, the first SAAF pilot to obtain the new ICAO Airline Transport Licence (ALTP) while still serving as a SAAF officer. They even allowed me to use one of our DC3 Dakotas on which I was instructing for my flying tests.

This book tells of how, on our way to the Sudan, when I hitch-hiked 2,000 miles by air and road from Nairobi to Johannesburg, to bring Kay and our three children back as a ferry pilot in a little Navion, we nearly lost our lives in storm conditions in Mozambique, and landed on a tiny grass airfield in the gloom of dusk. Minutes later we were in pitch darkness. On Kay's first night on a remote mission station in the South Sudan, our mud house was invaded by army ants. On the third night, our thatched roof caught fire and we only escaped with our lives, losing all our meagre possessions.

It is our story of those pioneering days. But I do touch on the amazing story of my American MAF colleague, Nate Saint, an ingenious pilot/engineer who, with four young American missionaries, attempted to reach the vicious Amazonian Auca people (as they were then called). The Aucas killed them all and great books have been written about that vain attempt to reach those jungle people. Now, fifty years later, two films have been made.

I also touch on the amazing story of how an American couple, Harvey and Lavina Hoekstra, who I used to fly in the the Sudan, crossed into Ethiopia and hacked their way with African helpers into a rain forest to reach one of Ethiopia's unreached tribes, called the Mesengos. They had been encouraged to do so by Emperor Haile Selassie. MAF played a great part in helping them, first by air drops of supplies and then later, when huge trees had been felled, were able to land where outsiders had never been before.

Those kind of stories can be told about MAF operations in many of the other remote countries in which MAF serves. It has been said that no other flying organisation lands at so many destinations as MAF. Often, remote ones where no other planes can reach, and where, to get to them in an hour or two in an MAF plane, might take many days of struggling through in four-wheel drive vehicles or on horse mule or even in some places on a camel.

I hope that readers of *Beaufighter Over the Balkans* will read my next book *From War to Peace* to catch the vision of turning 'weapons of war' into 'tools for peace', or as the Bible puts it – 'swords into ploughshares'.

MAF Headquarters produce regular news magazines and other informative and promotional literature. Below are the addresses of headquarters in English-speaking countries.

MAF United Kingdom
Castle Hill Avenue, Folkstone, CT20 2TN   Tel: (01303) 850950   Website: www.maf-uk.org

MAF Australia
PO Box 1099, Cairns, Queensland, 4870, Australia. Tel: +61 7 4046 1300 Website: www.maf.org.au

MAF Canada
PO Box 368, Guelph, Ontario, N1H 6K5, Canada Tel: +1 519 821 3914 Website: www.mafc.org

MAF New Zealand
PO Box 76-502, Manukau City 1702, Auckland, New Zealand
Tel: +64 9 262 1725 Website: www.maf.org.nz

MAF South Africa
PO Box 1288, Lanseria, Johannesburg, 1748, South Africa Tel: +27 11 6592880
Website: www.mafsa.co.za

MAF USA
PO Box 47, Nampa, Idaho 83653, USA   Tel: +1 208 498 0800 Website: www.maf.org

Index